Prefa

Ok, so I have to put something down here………..Nobody ever reads the preface, so why are you making me do it?……………...
stop rushing me I'm thinking…..
What does preface mean?..... According to Webster's dictionary.
Preface - *Something spoken as introductory to a discourse, or written as introductory to a book or essay; a proem; an introduction, or series of preliminary remarks*. So why not just say 'Introduction', I mean you don't go up to a work colleague and say "Can I preface my wife to you?"

In a way, it does sort of set up my book, because I am a grumpy old bo###ks, it's a natural male progression that comes with age, we can't help it and I do have a wee moan about things in this book….. just a tiny bit.
Also whilst I have your attention, can I just say, I'm not a writer, I am a story teller, so if I meet you in the street and you say "Oh I spotted three comas and two full stops missing, also page 63 fourth line down, that should have been a new paragraph" if you do, I'll probably break your nose, you can tell me you read it and its shite, that's fair enough, just don't correct me. I mean, I thought a *'colon'* was something in your body and a *'semi colon'* was, what was left after a surgeon had taken half your bowel out, I'm just saying I'm not a wordsmith.

Well what on earth made me think I could write a book.
They do say there is a book inside everybody and if truth be known that's where it should stop, and I'm sure some who read this will say the same about this book, for those of you who don't know me I had

a stroke in 2013 and whilst stuck in hospital I started writing about my hospital days on Facebook and found I enjoyed doing it. I also found when I read back on my notes it helped me see how far I had come.

Don't get me wrong, I never wanted a stroke but it has made me sit back, take stock of my life and lead me to a journey I would never have thought about taking, and along this journey I have met and befriended people I would normally have never had any reason to interact with, people who are now very precious to me.

I think it's made my outlook on life much stronger, instead of moaning and feeling sorry for myself, when it comes to undertaking a normal task like going for a swim or riding a bike, we sit down and we figure it out, and who is this 'we' I talk about, well it's a she and it's my wife Claire, for whom without, I would never have even got out of hospital let alone be driving myself around the country, I am privileged and proud to call her my wife and am very lucky to have the love she gives me, although if I can just qualify that last statement, there have been many times she would have killed me, maybe regretted it later but still killed me, I'm not the best patient in the world.

So, sit back, and I hope you enjoy my journey through life and thank you for taking the time to read my book.

JMcG

p.s. The front cover photo was taken in a Las Vegas hotel room after a good night at the tables, since my stroke memories have become very important to me and that was a hell of a night.

This book is dedicated to _____
                                  fill your name here

CH1
The 13 came to town

The embers were glowing, the comfort of the warmth as the fire gave her most, Claire beside me and our 2 dogs curled up on the rug enjoying the first heat from the open fire, "come on" I said, "let's do it outside".

I turned up the radio, we slipped out the door, leaving it open, just enough so we could still hear the music, we looked up, looked up as we have done many many times before, the hundreds, the thousands, nay the millions of stars stood over us twinkling through the dark night….10, 9, 8, rang out from inside, we turned we looked at each other….3, 2,1, HAPPY NEW YEAR.
 The cheers and music could be heard from the radio, then we heard voices, neighbours from other houses, a firework reached out into the darkened sky, then a second, we were no longer alone, as the houses around us came to life, 2012 was gone, now its 2013, little did we know then the changes this year would bring for us both.

We went back inside the cottage and settled down to finish our glass of wine and welcome in our friend 2013.

The number 13 has long been associated with bad luck…. but why?

It's just a number, how can it affect you, how did the two digits of 1 and 3 become such a fearful combination.
Researchers estimate that at least 10 percent of the U.S. population, that's more than 30 million people have a fear of the number 13, and to be even more specific the fear of Friday 13th, known as paraskevidekatriaphobia, results in financial losses in excess of $800 million annually, as people avoid marrying, traveling or in the most severe cases, even working. But what's so unlucky about the number 13, and how did this numerical superstition get started?

An early myth surrounding the origin of the fear involved one of the world's oldest legal documents, the Code of Hammurabi, which reportedly omitted a 13th law from its list of legal rules. In reality, the omission was no more than a clerical error made by one of the document's earliest translators, who failed to include a line of text—in fact, the code doesn't numerically list its laws at all.

Mathematicians and scientists, meanwhile, point to pre-eminence of the number 12, often considered a "perfect" number, in the ancient world. The ancient Sumerians developed numeral system based on the use of 12 that is still used for measuring time today; most calendars have 12 months; a single day is comprised of two 12-hour half days, etc.
Following so closely on the heels of a "perfect" number, some argue, the poor 13 was sure to be found lacking and unusual.
 This fear of the unknown would seem to play into two other popular theories for the number's unlucky connotation, both of which revolve around the appearance of a 13th guest at two ancient events: In the Bible, Judas Iscariot, the 13th apostle to arrive at the Last Supper, is the person who betrays Jesus.

Meanwhile ancient Norse lore holds that evil and turmoil were first introduced in the world by the appearance of the treacherous and mischievous god Loki, at a dinner party in Valhalla. He was the 13th guest, upsetting the balance of the 12 gods already in attendance. It also seems as if unexplained fears surrounding the number 13 are a primarily Western construct.

Some cultures, including the Ancient Egyptians, actually considered the number lucky, while others have simply swapped numbers as the base of their phobias—4 is avoided in much of Asia, for example. According to the Stress Management Centre and Phobia Institute in Asheville, North Carolina, more than 80 percent of hi-rise buildings in the United States, do not have a 13th floor, and the vast majority of hotels, hospitals and airports avoid using the number for rooms and gates as well.

Anyway back to the cottage, this was our bolt hole, its where we recharged our life's batteries.

Let me take you back in time, back to 2004, a time where everyone in Ireland was a millionaire, a time where we loved, and more unfortunately we believed our politicians, a time where Berti Ahern our wonderful political leader had his working class dark blue anorak surgically removed and a two thousand euro Armani suit grafted on in its place.

The country started going mad, we had more money in our pockets than we had ever had and people started spending like crazy.

Yes, I was drawn in to this monetary bubble and though a humble council worker, I went in search of my holiday home.

Myself and Claire had met later in life, we had both been previously married, divorced and our individual homes were established so the idea of a holiday home was not that crazy.

My father was from Glencolmcille, Co Donegal an area we both loved, so off we set in search of our little piece of paradise.

We looked at some 5 bedroom houses priced at a crazy 700,000 right down to a small cottage that still had several animals living in it.

This particular house made the national press under the Banner headline of

'IRELANDS CHEAPEST HOUSE'- I never thought to ask if the animals were included

After a few days of looking through numerous real estate agent's windows and talking to agents who continuously kept offering us 300% more than we wanted, Claire spotted an old cottage in the Donegal property news.

"That's it, that's what I'd like, an old traditional style cottage" as she looked at the tiny photo in the 2 inch add from one of the local property shops.

Off we went, to the town of Killybegs and into Henry Kees a local Auctioneer to enquire about this small cottage.

The Auctioneer dealing with the sale was not in the office and although we got the particulars the lady that gave them to us didn't know where its exact location actually was.

We travelled around the area checking all the for sale signs we could see but in reality it was the proverbial needle in the hay stack, so we decided to call it a day, get a shower, go down to the local pub and see if anyone there recognises it.

"Before we go back for a clean-up" I said "let me take you up to dad's old home place it's not far"
Claire nodded approval but there was a silent huff with the nod, the one that said, "I've just had enough"

  bullishly I drove on, through the village up the mountain, up to Kinakillew, I swung the car into an entranceway up over a small hill and stopped.

All this time as we journeyed, Claire was staring intensely at the property details we'd picked up from Killybegs an hour earlier.

"Well" I said, Claire broke her gaze from the sheet and looked up then all of a sudden started bouncing up and down in the seat,
" That's it" she screamed
"that's it, that's it, that's it", whilst at the same time shaking the estate agents paper in front of her.
She was right, there was the for sale sign in the window, dads old house up for sale, the very house he was born in.

I myself had not seen the house for over 35 years, even my own father when we showed him the estate agents details did not recognise it.
The thatch was on it the last time dad saw it, plus the way the photo was taken there was no land marks to see, just clear blue skies in the background, which, if you knew Donegal, clear blue skies is not your very first thought.
It was strange when we went to view it, the estate agent opened the door, I went in for the first time in over 35 years, it was different yet in my mind's eye I could still see my granny sitting on the right of the fire as you looked at it, grey hair tied up in a bun, black shawl

and black skirt, I don't remember her in anything but black.

I remembered the times we would sit there, dad and his brothers chatting away, mugs of tea in hand, a thick slice of homemade brown bread with butter and jam and in the middle of the floor was a pillow case full of Dilisk, for those who never came across it, Dilisk is a purple seaweed, harvested from the sea, dried in the outdoor sun and eaten much as you would a packet of salt flavoured crisps in my father's time.
I'm not sure about other coastal areas but in Glencolmcille when you went into a house the Dilisk would always make an appearance.

It was an acquired taste, you just reached into the pillow case, grabbed a handful then pulled at it, even today when I chew on a piece its distinguishing flavour takes me straight back to my childhood.

Anyway to cut a long story short, it took a year to complete the purchase but in 2005 the cottage returned to the family and eight years on there we were sitting in front of the open fire having toasted in 2013.

The cottage became a big part of our lives and still is to this day, January 1st 2013, I can say its seems another lifetime because it was.
Little did I know what lay ahead and how my life was going to not only change me, but also those dearest to me.

Ch2
MY Childhood and growth into stupidhood

I was never a skinny kid, I can remember as a young child my father drawing pictures on my belly with a biro. I used to be so proud of them and would constantly pull my shirt up and stick my belly out to all and sundry, I'm sure now it would probably be considered as abuse, but I loved it.

My first school was called Corpus Christy in Bordsley Green, I can actually remember the first day at school and leaving my mother at the front gate. We were lined up in front of the main door, then told to walk on, I turned looking at my mother she was looking but she never waved, I welled up, tears in my eyes but I held them back, I didn't want to cry in front of my new school mates.

My brother, being 3 years older was already settled in to the routine at school and had told me stories of this unknown institution,
We entered into the class room, one side of the room had a big poster running down the length of the room, it had the alphabet on it, each letter was beside a picture of an item which started with that letter. i.e. A was for apple, B was for ball etc. We learned it as a phonetic alphabet so for example the letter D would be Duh, the letter A would be Ahh.
Each morning this was our first job of the day the teacher Mrs. McDonald would point at each letter with a long stick and we would all shout out in unison the letter and what it was for.

Back to my first day and my horrible brother, I was sitting at a table next to a boy called Timothy Touhy, the teacher came around with some small chalk boards in a wooden frame, and now we reach the part my horrible brother was responsible for. The teacher handed out what I now understand to be unrefined lumps of chalk, only my wonderful older sibling had told me it was dried out dog pooh.
The lump of dog pooh was left on the table in front of me, I watched as the other children all picked up the dog pooh and started to write on the chalk board, looking back I now realise this was the first time I encountered peer pressure because reluctantly I reached out picked up my piece of dog pooh and started to scribble away and was quite impressed how well dog pooh worked, it was some days later after I had got to know a few people that I mentioned my thoughts on the chalk and was put right in front of a giggling class.

There was a neighbour down the road whose mother used to take it in turns with our mother to take us to school. Her boys where called Richard and Tony, Richard was in the same class as me and we soon became friends finding a similar interest in cars, which I suppose considering his surname was Vann it was no great shock. Come the break times when most of the others were running around like headless chickens, Richard and I had our faces glued to the railings watching the cars going past, seeing who could recognise the make and model first.
I later on (2012) found Richard again on Facebook, well actually he found me, my memory from school that he too was one of the fat kids, only to find he'd grown into a right skinny bastard whilst I still had the rolls.
He was a musician, as was I and although it had been some 40 years since we last met we had other things in common, prior to

finding Richard on face book I also came across another old Corpus Christi school buddy Barbara Close, or as I knew her Barbara Marklew, I have to say with the abuse Facebook sometimes gets its been terrific to come across these old school chums although calling Barbara a chum might be pushing it, you have to remember we were aged 5 and in junior school, until we reached the grand old age of 11, even though I kind of fancied Barbara at that age you did not say that to your school pals, as girls where yuk. She hung out with a Blonde haired girl called Anita Carroll who was the pretty girl in school although a bit up her own you know what.

Barbara also became a musician and still looks very much as she did at school and is happily living on the isle of Wight, making a name for herself with a camera, she has one of those really good looking active husband whose idea of fun is to attach his surf board to a parachute and not satisfied with catching a wave he then catches the wind and reaches for the sky, oh and did I mention he has a really cool job lots of dosh and good looking. I just can't think what they call people like him, so maybe it was with good reason that I didn't pursue Barbara, I don't have a head for heights, when I stand on a surf board it sinks and the size of parachute I'd need would leave half the Isle of Wight in darkness.

My time in junior school was not a bad one, but I do remember one incident with a teacher Mrs. Keating, our class was going on some sort of day trip and the teachers were packing the kids into their own cars, Mrs. Keating pulled up in her car, stood by the car shouting, "Plenty of room with me" her car was an old Ford Prefect, nobody made a move and continued to try and get into the other teacher's cars at which point I said "Nobody wants to get in your car miss".

She slammed the open car door, made a bee line directly to me grabbed my hand, pulled me back into the school, into a class room, closed the door, then smacked the back of my legs with all her might, only stopping to pick up a ruler, slap my hand and then my bum.

This was nearly 50 years ago but I can still see her face as she continued to hit me, I was six years old, she pulled me back to the car bundled me in, I can't remember if anyone else came with us but we drove to the venue and I was told to remain in the car and be quiet. I don't know if Mrs. Keating is still alive but I think she was the first person that ever brought the emotion of hate into my life. I have no idea what happened to her and frankly I don't care.

From my junior school, I passed my eleven plus exam and was accepted into St Phillips school, it was a Grammar school in Edgbaston, Birmingham, I had a fairly mundane school career, I wasn't the brightest of pupils and if I'm honest I managed to completely mess up any chance I had of coming out of there with any sort of qualification and ashamedly I was only known for the longest single period of truancy in the school's history, probably still hold this record as a few years after I left, the school became a 6th form college and I left with one O level (Ordinary level) in music.

I did get a job though and my dreams of being a lay about dosser where dashed, it was with a company called 'Jones and Crossland'

Jones and Crossland was a very popular musical instruments shop in the mid too late 1960's.
It was situated on Smallbrook Queensway roughly where Richer Sounds are now.

A visit there on a Saturday afternoon would often result in seeing well-known local musicians.
Park musical equipment was stocked there and it was said by many people at the time that Cleartone Musical Instruments, who made Park, were owned by the same people as the shop.

Apart from the brand name on the front the 100 watt and 50 watt Park valve amps, and the 4/12 Park speaker cabinets were almost indistinguishable from Marshall equipment, and it was rumored that Park had been born out a need to fill a gap left by a contract to manufacture Marshall equipment, which had come to an end.
Rumor also suggested that Park was basically Marshall circuitry with minor changes to avoid patent infringement.
It is certainly true that on inspection of the innards the only obvious difference without reference to a parts list, was that Park used pairs of the large KT66 valves in push-pull manner (one pair in the 50 watt amp and two pairs in the 100 watt amp), whilst the Marshall equipment of the time used the more compact KT88 valves in the same manner.

The maiden name of the wife of Jim Marshall's friend Johnny Jones wife was said to be Park, so there is probably some truth in those rumors.
There was also a range of Park Guitars.
Park was eventually acquired by Marshall. The Jones and Crossland shop closed some years ago.

So my first job after leaving school was at Jones and Crosslands repair shop, a small little workshop in Legge Lane, in the jewelry quarter in Birmingham, still a very well-known area of Birmingham today.

The front door was a security door because we did hold quite a large amount of Gold leaf, used in decorating some of the instruments.

I met a number of celebrities whilst working there, the doorbell would go, I'd take a peek through the spy hole, I don't really know why I bothered unless they had striped shirts, a black eye mask and a bag that said swag, I just let them in.

I didn't always recognize the celebrity in the flesh so to speak, Richard Baker, he was a news reader on the BBC, a very accomplished flute player, James Galway, the man with the Golden Flute, that means something totally different in Dublin, when I heard the names the penny dropped as to who they were, but one day the bell went, I checked the peep hole, no mask's so I let them in, one chubby bullish man who was obviously in charge, he looked at me "Go fetch your boss" for a split second I stood there, "well go on then, go and fetch him" off I toddled, Paul the manager was on the polishing machine which was rather noisy, I went up to him and shouted "Customer to see you," Paul nodded and mouthed 'five minutes' whilst also holding up five fingers.

I went back to the front office, the gentlemen had made themselves comfortable on the leather seating, I told the man, Paul would be there in 5 minutes, he suddenly jumped up and he started going a bit red and with a contorted face he yelled at me, "Don't you know who I am". What was I to-do, it was one of those moments in life you dread, I honestly had no idea who he was and sheepishly in a low voice I said "No", he then said, "My Name is Kenny Ball, now go and tell your boss I'm waiting, "NOW" he yelled, I scuttled out of the office, Paul was still on the machine, "It's Mr. Ball" I shouted the machine drowning out my words, I pushed the stop button, Paul looked angrily at me "He said to say his name is Mr. Ball", "Mr. Ball",

Paul repeated "Yes" I said "Mr. Kenny Ball," Paul immediately turned, pulled off his polishing apron and headed out.

I later found out there was a TV band Kenny Ball and his Jazz men, that must have been the little fella's that were with him

Not all the celebrities were ignorant, one day Alvin Stardust called up with some of his band, he was really cool and was wearing black leather trousers and jacket (A singer from the 70's) My biggest surprise was when I answered the door to Roy Wood.

Roy**Wood** (born 8 November 1946 is an English singer-songwriter and multi-instrumentalist. He was particularly successful in the 1960s and 1970s as member and co-founder of the Move, The Electric Light Orchestra and Wizard As a songwriter, he contributed a number of hits to the repertoire of these bands.

He worked for Jones and Crossland many years previous and was a pal of Paul's, Paul had been polishing and Mr. Wood grabbed an apron and started polishing some saxophone key's whilst having great chats peppered with laughter, with Paul, I was just standing there mesmerised.

Paul switched the polisher off Roy's eyes lit up "Lunchtime?" he looked at Paul who said yep, "Is the café still open" asked Roy and with a nod of yes the three of us headed over to the greasy spoon, now for those that don't know Roy Wood he had a close resemblance to Hagrid from Harry Potter, a face that was only just distinguishable through the mass of hair and beard and when we entered the café, heads turned and the usual verbal buzz suddenly went up several decibels but after a few moments it all quitened down to where it started, I think there was an obvious recognition of Roy followed by a "Sure what the F##ck would he be doing here," meanwhile 3 full greasy fries where delivered to the table, I normally had to pay for my lunch but this day it was bought for me by Roy

Wood, I should put it on a T-shirt, he was a really down to earth nice guy, you should learn from that Kenny Ball you ignorant pig.

I mentioned Marshall amps earlier during the 70's and 80's there wasn't a major band on the planet that was not using Marshall amps Jim Marshall called into our work shop in Legge lane as his own place was next door, just to fill you in, this is where we repaired and refurbished all types of Brass and Woodwind instruments.

It was an interesting and varied craft, we even took the bend out of a Tenor sax to make what they called a stritch, it's not as easy as it may sound the overall length of the instrument had to be exactly the same or the pitch would be different, the key arrangement was also fiddly but the finished article looked superb.

Anyway back to Jim Marshal, he called in one day and was given the cleanest mug and he joined us for our Tea break, regaling lots of stories and I'm sure some tall tales but I do believe this tale was true.

He was spending a lot of time in Australia and he had his Rolls Royce shipped over from the UK.

He went on to tell the story of how the rear axle failed, he contacted Rolls Royce they sent a team of technicians and a new axle and Jim was soon back on the road in his own car, he returned to the UK along with his prized motor vehicle and some months past when he thought about his car problems in Oz, he asked his secretary if any correspondence had been received from Rolls Royce regarding the repair but none had arrived.

He then asked her to write and request an invoice for the work so he could square it with his insurance only for him to receive a letter a week later along the lines of

Dear Mr Marshall,

  you recently wrote to us regarding a problem with the rear axle of your car, I'm afraid we are at a loss to your request for an invoice for a replaced rear axle, Rolls Royce axles never fail and I can only think you are getting mixed up with some other vehicle.

We thank you for your recent correspondence.

Regards

Peter Ward

Managing Director.

I don't know how true it was but as a young 17-year-old I hung on every word he said.

After I left Jones and Crossland I went to Weaman Motors, this is where I learned to be a panel beater and paint sprayer, not much to mention from my time here except I used to get a lift home from Johnny Riggs a wanna be hells angel who was one of the mechanics, he had a cool BSA bike but he also owned a Bond Bug, you should look them up on you tube.
It could be driven on a motor bike license with a 700cc engine 4 speed gear box and only came in one colour, orange, it cost £629.00 new which in today's terms would be £14,000.00, you lifted the front canopy up and sat into it, well nearly lying down in it, it was a brilliant ride even though it wasn't the fastest vehicle around the

seating position gave you the experience of travelling at light speed, and talking of light speed Tom Carron the man who designed it was contacted by George Lucas and asked to help turn the Bug into a land speeder in the first Star Wars movie.
Do you remember the scene where the young Luke Skywalker along with C3PO raced across the desert in the landspeeder, well, that was a Bond Bug with a false body and a mirror along the bottom to give the effect of it hovering?

After a few years I moved on to another repair shop, I can't think of its name but it was based in Aston in a building that was formerly the stables for the Ansell's Brewery, 3 men were joint owners of the company, Ken, Bob and Charlie, Bob was the only man I ever met that could light an Oxy Acetylene torch from a cigarette, the acetylene would not light from the fag you needed just the right amount of oxygen mixed in and when correct the torch would suddenly burst in to life with a six inch flame shooting from it, now remember a cigarette was not very long and after seeing Bob do this once or twice it made sense of why his flat cap how so many scorch marks on the peak.
Ken was a real nice guy who treated me well and could well have sacked me over this next incident.

As I said earlier the building used to be a stables so it was a long thin narrow building, the old stable part was the body shop with the spray booth at the top end so it was a bit of a nuisance when you wanted to get a car out because you had to move a number of cars in the body shop first in order to get out the finished car.
So one day I had completed the paintwork to a car and asked Richie to give me a hand moving the cars, we only had to move the ones in the middle this would have been the walk way in to the

stables for the horses, the area left and right of the walk way where the stables once were still had cars that where been worked on, eventually it was clear to drive my car out, I started to reverse out only to hear Richie screaming at me, I felt a bit of a bump like I'd gone over a speed bump but took no notice, I looked up the workshop to see Richie frozen to the spot, his hands on his head, I just thought maybe I had left some tape and masking paper on the car so I stopped put it in first and drove back down to the paint shop, Richie ran towards me screaming something unintelligible, I felt the same bump again and watched as Ritchie hands on head, went down on to his knees.

I got out of the car and in complete innocence said to Ritchie "What's the matter", Ritchie moved his hands down, came up to me, put both hands on my shoulder, his face not three inches from my face and said "Not only did you reverse over Charlie's legs you then stopped and drove forward over them again". Ahh now I knew what the bumps were.

As it happened because Charlie didn't see me coming he didn't tense up and the hospital said that's what saved him getting any real damage apart from some bruising but the worst was yet to come, I went into Ken's office like a lamb walking into the slaughter house, he had heard and just said "Sit" and he went off down the shop, he was only gone a few minutes but it was an eternity, I was going through my head what I would tell mom and dad about losing my job.

Ken came back into the office, his wife who was the secretary was sitting at her desk. "He'll live, said Ken," then in a mumbled voice "more's the pity", his wife put her hand on her mouth to muffle her laughter, then Ken looked at me "what's up with you" he said, Nervously   I asked "am I in trouble"

"you ought to be" said Ken "You ran him over twice and both times you managed to miss his f###ing head" his wife just burst out laughing, I was trying not to laugh I still wasn't sure if I was ok or if I was going to be sacked but with the two of them laughing it was too much and I cracked up, by this time two or three other lads had come into the office I often thought what the Ambulance men thought as they strapped Charlie onto a stretcher to take him out and all the loud laughter coming from the office.

I had some good times there but the country went into a depression, the coalminers strike meant we could only work a three-day week due to the power cuts.

Ken pulled me aside one day and told me he had to let me go, it was a sad day, I loved working there.

Through the early years of my life up to my late teens even though I was plumper than most lads I think the amount of activity I was involved with i.e. football, rugby, cycling etc. kept the weight off me, although I do remember buying a pair of wrangler jeans and in the 70's they used to have the waist and leg length on the wrangler patch at the back of the jeans, I took some abuse when one of my mates spotted my waist was 32 inches, boy, what I'd give now for a 32-inch waist.

In the early 80's I started to get big getting up to 18 stone, this was when I started my never ending up and down life of dieting.

I had some strange diets, I remember my father coming home with this sheet of paper he got from a buddy at work, it consisted of a boiled egg diet, eating about 4 boiled eggs a day, I was on it a few weeks and I know my memory is not what it used to be but I swear I didn't go to the loo for a bloody fortnight.

I suppose in reality the activity your involved in during your teenage years burns lots of energy, cycling, sports, all the normal teen things but as you get older that all changes.

I developed a diet of my own….. No alcohol, cornflakes for breakfast, no midday meal, then when I got home in the evening I had four large sausages, full tin of Heinz baked beans, had to be Heinz, and 2 slices of toast, it might be a dietician's nightmare but it worked for me and I lost nearly 5 stone, hitting the scales at 13 stone 5 pounds.
So as the years passed my weight would slip up then either the lack of clothing choice or a major function such as getting wed would spur me into another diet, this pattern continued up into my 40's but I'd noticed as I got older the weight was harder to shift but I did seem to remain at a weight which was more than it should have been but not morbidly obese.

By this time, I was married for a second time and living in Ireland and not in a happy place, so I left my wife Karen, expected to basically spend the latter years of my life as a single man.
They do say 'you'll find what you want when you stop looking for it,' and if they didn't well I'm saying it now.

I stopped looking and before you know it Claire was in my life, everything changed I became happy and I mean really happy for the first time in years.
   On our first date we met up in a carpark in Tuam as arranged then headed into Galway, although I was separated from Karen we were not divorced.
   Tuam has been my home for over 20 years and I enjoy living here but the one thing it's great for is gossip.

The way I felt I couldn't give a shite what folk said about me but Claire was from a well-known Tuam family, so our first few dates were sort of clandestine occasions, driving into Galway City and taking long walks along Salthill prom…… Hold on a cotton-picking minute MCGINLEY going for long walks… It must be love.

We would be texting constantly to each other and on occasions she would ask me to call around when it was dark, no not because she was ashamed of me, although I have done a few things since…… Ahh…. I'll leave that for another book, it was because of the local gossip that is guaranteed in Tuam that I used the cloak of darkness to get to know my lady better.

Well this one night I went a calling, not turning up empty handed as I had two bottles of wine accompanying me, so anyway we chatted whilst listening to music on MTV, we snuggled up together on the couch sipping our wine, next thing I remember was been woken by Claire shouting at me, it was about 2.00am "What are you doing here, get out, get out", I jumped up trying to calm her but whatever way she woke she was having none of it, I was trying to get my shoes on with Claire still in this agitated state, I got my shoes and jacket on, opened the front door and it was pissing down and I mean torrential, I turned looked at Claire saying "You wouldn't put a dog out on a night like this", all I heard was "OUT" and I was gone heading home in the worst storm I had ever seen, rain was flowing down the roads right up to kerb level, eventually I got back to my flat, I may well have just gone swimming fully clothed, I could not have been wetter.

Did I just slip into the warm clean, dry bed…? No……. I wrote a song and a couple of years later it appeared on my first album, it's called 'Going home in the pouring rain,' a couple of nights later Claire called around to my flat, "I've written a new song" I said, "oh lets hear it then" she answered.   I was only half way through the first chorus when she just burst out laughing, came up gave me a hug saying, "No one's ever written a song about me before", I didn't burst her bubble, by telling her I was really pissed off with her when I wrote it.

Well I don't know how long it was but it was a long time since I felt contentment like this and with contentment came an appetite and I ballooned up to a massive 24 stone, complaining to Claire that she was shrinking my shirts in the tumble drier, I went from a XL shirt up to a 5XL content each time the extra XL i.e. 2XL to 3XL etc. fitted around my bulk.
I didn't need to be fed to win my heart but that didn't stop me filling my gob with all the foods I should have avoided.

Eventually I had to admit my size to myself and along with Claire, I joined a local Gym in Claregalway, it was going ok, I always complained at going but although I never admitted this to Claire I got a good feeling after a hard session, it's all about those little things in the brain, pheromones or something similar, the staff at the gym were fabulous and always encouraging, I got to know them well and even today Brenda, Catriona and Leona are lovely people that I can call my friends.

Then one day things changed, the three girls decided they were going to do a half marathon, Claire decided she was going to join them.
I thought this a great idea although I could see a lot of hard work ahead for Claire.
Claire had no problem walking the dogs anything up to 7 miles but had never tried running.
I decided this could be a chance to raise a few bob for the Galway

Hospice and approached some of the contractors that were doing works for the council that I was overseeing and got a good response, one of the contractors was called Shareridge Ltd owned by Mick McNamara, he was a real character and I know he won't mind me telling you some of his story.

Mick was a very hard working man and built up a very successful business but although he worked hard he also partied hard and due to the demon drink he lost it all, but that wasn't the end of mick he cleaned himself up went to AA got of the gargle and rebuilt his business, he has one of those infectious personalities that you can't help but love the guy and even as I write this I haven't seen mick in years but if I rang him tomorrow we would talk for hours.

He treated his work force with great respect, he might pull up to the job in an old van or in an Audi A8 either way you would find him 10 minutes later down a trench up to his knees in mud, actually I think this was when mick was at his happiest.

He had lost faith to a certain degree as to the work ethic of some Irish workers and whilst looking for labour he encountered some Russian guys, some from Russia others from former Russian states, he had a group of about 10 lads and bought an old run down farm and set them up in there.

Their work ethic was very much like that of the Irish in my father's time, they worked to send money home to their families and minded and looked out for each other, they bought pigs for the farm then one of the lads who was a butcher slaughtered a pig and butchered it up giving them a cheap source of food, they also had other animals including chickens and the likes, also growing their own produce, they were hard working lads who minded their equipment as they understood the better the machinery worked the better it was for them.

Anyway back to my story, I told mick about Claire doing the half marathon and with a wry smile on his face mick looked at me…." I'll tell you now what I'll do Jon mcGinley, I'll give you 200 euro's if you do the run".
"No mick" I said "it's not me its Claire that's doing the run".
"And I'm telling you" says mick "you do it……200 euro's" he holds out his hand rubbing his fingers on the imaginary 200 quid, I couldn't say no and so began my journey to my first half marathon.

I was not stupid enough to think I could run it, but there was no rule saying you couldn't walk it.

I walked around my local park just gently trying to get my fitness level up, I would just walk for an hour I never really knew what distance I was going so myself and Claire measured out a walk close to our home it was 5km in distance and one day I set off on my walk eventually getting back home, falling into the armchair exhausted, it was only then that it dawned on me, I would have to go around another 3 times and even then I would not be quite finished but because I have a big gob and had told everyone I knew including posts on Facebook telling all I was doing a half marathon, I had no option but to press on.

Slowly but surely my fitness improved, and my weight was going down but more importantly my distance had improved and I was now walking up to 15 km.

Claire and myself went out to Achill Island and walked part of the route about a week before, then the day arrived we headed off early that morning driving to the island, I had never done this before so was unsure as what to expect.

The adrenalin rushes you get as the time clocks down to the start is something I had never experienced before, it's that sort of feeling when you start talking complete gibberish, but it was ok as most of the people were the same.

I have to say the organisation was excellent, we parked up went in with our registration sheets and came back out with a small gym bag, with a few energy drinks and biscuits and a water bottle, oh yes and the all-important number and chip that had your details on, you tied it on to your shoe then as you passed the timing gate it registered your time and details.
We met up with the girls, handing around jars of Vaseline, rubbing it on the insides of our legs, I found a quite spot out of the way of the ladies and also covered my bits in the Vaseline so as to stop any chance of chaffing.
The chatter was busy amongst us; it was a nervous chatter no one really knowing what quite to expect.
The girls made their way closer to the front whilst I hung around towards the back with maybe a few hundred people behind me.

The start was announced, the gun went off and we were on our way, a surge of people just passed me in an instance, I fought back and managed to pass some of them out but their pace was too quick for me and slowly I slipped further and further back, I was amazed when we reached the first portaloo a queue of about 20 girls were huddled around it, we had only gone about 2.0km, I heard one of them later talking about it she said it was all down to nerves.

Slowly, one by one the kilometres passed, the route was out from Keel, back towards Achill sound then turning at Bunacurry, and around the back of the island towards Dugart I noticed some people getting into cars, their efforts defeated, all through the day a motor bike was circling the route with a paramedic on board each time as he passed me he would slow down and shout "Are you ok", I'd just smile and give him the thumbs up, there were people stationed at any road junction to make sure you didn't go in the wrong direction, I was surprised at how many youngsters had given up their day to help, the same could be found at all the water stations, they had great encouragement to all taking part.

When you go around the back, around towards Dugart it seems like you have been transported to another reality, the views are stunning, I have to say this helped me immensely as it took my mind off my sore feet.

Eventually you get to within about 5km from the end point only to be greeted by a major hill, the climb was hard, the back of my legs were burning but then it came into view the end the summit I'd made it butttttt, Ahhhhh no just as you get to the top you realise it isn't, it's just a short gentle downward slope and then the climb begins again, I have to say it was the only time I genuinely thought of quitting but gladly I didn't, and eventually I reached the top of the climb and Port came into view, I could see the finish, my heart skipped a beat as I continued on, then the familiar sound of the paramedics motor bike echoed behind me, the volume soaring as he approached, I readied myself for his now familiar question "Are you ok" only to see him blast past me, horn blowing whilst shaking a fist of victory in the air.

My victory, I could see it, just meters away, I passed the pub in Port and my friends were all there cheering away with pints in their hands spilling over the glass as they roared me in, my god, I thought, I'm going to sink some beers to celebrate, Claire met me and walked the last hundred meters with me, I did it I finished The Achill Island half marathon….. and I wasn't the last finisher there were 4 other people who finished after me plus over 100 people dropped out over the day.

After dreaming of those beers I didn't need them I was as high as a kite, then my head started spinning, Claire came over to me sat me down and rushed off coming back a few minutes later with water and a sandwich, pushing them into my hand "Here," she said "get these down you, you are suffering from dehydration." It was a good half hour before I could get up and walk and by this time the lactic acid had really built up in my legs and each step was agony but worth it, we all cleaned up and headed out for food and beer.

We landed in to the local Chinese restaurant, we were shown to a table and once more the drinks were flowing, I don't think there was anything more than 7 seconds of silence amongst us as we laughed the whole night through, I really am blessed with my friends.

But eventually the hunger grew and grew, we were no longer hungry, we were famished, the restaurant was not prepared for the crowds and the waiters ran around the place like headless chickens, I think it's quite an acquired skill when as a waiter you can pass 20 or 30 people trying to get your attention and yet not see a single diner in the place.

So Brenda, now can I first explain, the lovely Brenda is a small framed 5 foot nothing wee blonde creature or as we say in Ireland Crayture, but as petite as she maybe I wouldn't pick an argument with her, Brenda got up, marched into the kitchen, I would love to say we then heard the crashing of pans and smashing of plates but it didn't happen that way, the serving doors opened, out popped Brenda, she came back to the table "that's sorted" she said and low and behold food arrived at our table, as the dishes hit the table people started laying claim to the food, I'm not sure if we ate what we ordered but it didn't matter, it was soakage and we badly needed it.

I wanted to keep the health train going and continued my gym regime using the pool, not only to swim but as it was a level pool, four foot and a few inches deep, I would run up and down the lanes as a low impact form of exercise.
I found these sessions great for thinking and mulling over ideas, then an idea came into my head.
"What about running a marathon in the pool?"
Brenda and Catriona thought I was nuts but that's ok and nothing new, if I remember right it worked out about at just over 2,100 lengths of the pool, I started to get excited, I contacted the Guinness Book of world records to see if they would consider it for inclusion in their book but after a long wait I got an answer back telling me if they took my efforts and recorded it as a bench mark, there were too many variables that could differ from pool to pool i.e. depth of pool, length of pool etc. and although they wished me well they would not be able to consider it for inclusion in their publication.

This I have to say dampened my enthusiasm and although I did say I would do it, I never got around to it before my stroke.

I needed a new challenge and it wasn't long coming around, 'The Lough Corrib Cycle'
A cycle route that took you out of Galway city on towards

Connemara around to Headford and back into Galway.

There was a choice of a 46km section or the full 120km route, of cause with my bravado I insisted we do the 120km.

Ch3….. I'm putting the band back together (Jake Blues)

So the half marathon crew got back together and training began for this new challenge.
Now the saying goes "It's as easy as riding a bike" and yes riding a bike was easy but what they don't tell you, and I'm up for correction but I'm sure I haven't heard a saying along the lines of

"And after 25 miles yer ass will be burning"

Every one of us were suffering from bottom burn, as the saddles tortured us in the early days.
I scoured the internet looking for a big wide soft saddle that would be kind to my now red rear.
Then I read a piece that explained why saddles on racing bikes resembled a torture implement from the dark ages, it was all to do with friction, the less saddle that interacted with your botty, the less friction caused, the less friction caused, the less problem so instead of getting a big wide comfy saddle I opted for a narrow hard black polished one.
Did this solve my problem…. Did it feck…. The saddle in question was designed for the sleek animal like cyclist that think nothing of a quick 100 miles before breakfast, and not the overweight thick ass of an aging idiot like me.

Training continued and to be fair my ass became a lot more tolerant allowing me to cycle distances of 60 to 65 km, but eventually the weekend arrived, we had met the day before at a function that I can't remember what is was for, I think it might have been Leona's daughter's communion, anyway the weather forecast was brutal and we debated whether we would go ahead with the cycle, coming to the conclusion that as we had raised monies on the promise of taking part then we would do the 46km route and then retire to the pub.

Bikes checked over, tyre pressures checked and rechecked, Vaseline liberally smeared to places no one can talk about, and off we started, heading into miserable cold and wet weather (just a normal Galway summer).
Claire and Brenda went off at a decent pace whilst I hung back and was accompanied by Catriona, she said she was just keeping me company but I know really she needed my guidance to help her along, woo look a pink Elephant just floated past my window.

I was quite taken aback by the so called regular cyclists, they cycled in packs and as they approached you from behind they just screamed "LEFT" and expected everyone to pull tight into the left hand side of the road, they would stick their arms out and push you if you were not over far enough for their liking even to the point where I saw them push one young lad off his bike into the grass verge, complete tossers who thought they were something special.

The weather and especially the wind was making the journey harder than any of the training I had done, I was on some serious hills heading down and you have to remember I am a large weight, yet we all found ourselves having to cycle downhill, now that's just bloody unfair.

Eventually Mamm came into view, I could see the other cyclists and my heart lifted as I knew my torture was coming to an end.

I reached a spot were there must have been 100 bikes or more, I added mine to the collection then went off in search of my women.

I spotted Claire coming down the road towards me carrying tea and a sandwich which I very happily accepted, 2 gulps of lovely warm tea, "Where are the girls" I asked, Claire motioned and I followed her over to find Brenda and Catriona enjoying their tea and sandwich.

"Thank god that's over" says I, then I looked at Brenda, I knew by the look on her face, "you're going to carry on aren't you" I said, Brenda's face, contorted, smiled and grimaced whilst looking sheepish all at the same time, eventually she said "Ah sure I'll give it a lash", I looked straight at Catriona, she broke eye contact and looked at the ground, "Well feck ya's, cos I'm not doing it" and I took another bite of my sandwich at the same time looking at Claire, I knew from her face,

"Ahh, Jaysus, not you too" I said.

Claire looked at me, "I'll not go if you don't want to go on".

I was so pissed off, I just sat down to finish my sandwich and drink, I didn't want to be the cop out, it had been my idea, I'll have to do it, but how, I was feeling drained, then as I finished my tea I heard many of the other cyclists all saying the same thing, "That's the hard bit over, we have the wind at our backs now, sure we'll fly it" not just once but several times I heard the same thing said, I began to think maybe I could do it.

"Claire" she looked over, I said "come on then let's give it a lash, if I don't make it I can always get the bus", there was a bus that followed the tour and would pick up those who found themselves unable to go on, but I really didn't want to have to catch the bus of shame.

We headed off and I have to say the lads were right the wind was at our backs and I was moving along at quite a decent pace, I didn't mind hills because if you go up, you have to come down, I remember watching as the better cyclists who eased passed me with no effort on some of the climbs, but 5 minutes later I would zoom past them, I was going to say because of my weight but remembering my physics from college it was because I had more kinetic energy than them………. Ok, it was because I was fat.
One of the hills was like a spiralling snake, turning as it went up, you could only see to the next bend and could not be sure when it would end, I was getting slower and slower, I was now below walking pace, "I can't go on", I said out loud, head starring down at the ground, the decision was made, I would get to the next bend and get off the bike, there was no shame in it, I had passed a number of bikers walking on the way up, anyway I reached the bend and was just about to dismount when I looked up and there was Claire, waiting for me but more importantly she was on level ground, yes the hill was beaten, I had made it, we had a little breather then headed on to the next town Corna Mona, do I mention it because it's a world famous village?
Because it's on the World Heritage list?
No I mention this very famous Irish village because it had a tea and coffee stop with hundreds of homemade cakes.
We dismounted our bikes, now you have to remember I was doing this to try and lose weight, I looked at the cake through the eyes of a three-year-old, going from tray to tray and a big puss because I knew I couldn't indulge myself.
Claire looked at me "go on then" she said "you deserve one."

So I had my cake and ate it.

We continued on, by this time Claire was happy enough that I would complete the course so by the time we got to Headford we split up with herself heading off on her own.
I actually found this last section, approx. 30km, to be the hardest, mainly because it was on the flat all the way.
You see even though hills can be tough the downward slopes offer you the chance to stand up on the pedals and rest that very sensitive part of your body otherwise known as yer Bum.

A group of 6 lovely ladies passed me out, as the last one passed me she rode up level with me asking if I was ok, which I thought was very sweet, so I asked could I tag on the back and cycle with them.
It's quite amazing how much easier it is to ride if you are drafting, I've seen it on the TV when the Tour De France is on, you see the teams cycling to the front whilst their sprinter specialist stays tucked in behind the group conserving his energy, and it really does work, the girls allowed me to conserve energy and the next 10km racked up pretty quickly, then with about 10km left the girls decided to stop for a break, I had got to that point where I knew if I stopped I would not get going again, I shouted thanks to them, wished them well and with a wave I was passed them and all on my own again.

I reached a section of the road I knew really well as my house in Galway was close by, more importantly I knew where the downward sections were so as to give my beloved ass a break.
I passed the road that took me down to my house, I was now so close, then I started laughing out loud, I don't know was it some

kind of nervous reaction but when I tried to stop I couldn't and was now laughing out loud like some kind of eejit.

There it was, the road, the island junction that took me to the Menlo Park Hotel, the finishing point, I quickly debated in my mind whether I should go around the island as per the highway code and decided Feck it, I crossed the road onto the pavement saving me an an extra 100m pulled up in the carpark of the hotel…………." I DID IT"

Claire was waiting for me and we headed in to wondrous applause and cheers…… No we didn't, we went in and a chap said "Fair play to ya, well done" gave me a photo copied A4 sheet that said 'This is to confirm that Blank space (you had to fill your own name in) has completed the Tour De Corrib in aid of Croi Ireland.

I didn't care, in my own heart I had set myself a challenge and had completed it, we caught up with the girls before we left both had similar botty complaints but hey ho, c'est la vie.

I wouldn't say that exercising was a passion for me, but I did have a passion and it was music, now I could have approached this in many different ways, I could have studied music or I could have taught music but that wasn't where my heart was, what I wanted was to perform it.

I don't consider myself an extrovert but I suppose there must be a trace in there as and I'm sure all performers will admit this, even if not out loudly, but the enjoyment of performing is then enhanced when you finish as it would be in my case a song, by the feedback you get, the applause, the cheers, it becomes your food, as the saying goes it feeds your ego, does that make me egotistical, I don't know and don't care, I just wanted to get that word into my book as it makes me appear intelligent.

So the music, I played a bit in the UK but it was harder there, a big city like Birmingham, the music was very much in the city centre and it was a hard scene to break into, places like the Rum Runner a bar where Duran Duran were resident, you might get a 10 to 15 min set, whilst the big boys were massaging their ego's, don't get me wrong, they were ok you could talk to them but it was very much a us and them like situation and that was similar across the city. Birmingham had a really big vibrant scene and although there were a lot of doors 99% of them were locked and closed.

So when it came to making regular money from singing, it was down to busking.
    Now busking might to some seem an easy thing to do but it did have its problems, firstly the shop owners, sometimes they would send out their security staff to shift you on and the security guys all had one thing in common, either they had failed the police entry exams or too fat to pass the medical, you would be in the middle of a song and all of a sudden Lurch's two ugly brothers would start pushing you down the road whilst a third would give a few kicks to yer guitar case sending everything flying including your money.

Then there were the real cops, sometimes they would leave you alone, it would depend on their mood and how busy they were.

But the most dangerous could be another musician, especially if he thought you were on his pitch.
I am and never was a violent man but I am stubborn and when someone told me to move on it sometimes took the introduction of a blade into the conversation before I would come to my senses and move along.

You could make decent money if you had the right pitch and the elements were in your favour, not sure why but people stuck their hands in their pockets more often in nice sunny weather.
Also Christmas was a great time, in the 80's a half decent job, which I had, could pay you £40 to £50 a day, but, if I hit the right spot and the shoppers were in a good mood, I could make £60 to £70 a day doing something I really loved.
You never let the pot build up too much, during song breaks you would empty the big coins out of the bag, 2 reasons for this, if the crowd sees a big pot of money they are less likely to give and secondly and I found this out the hard way, if some dick head grabs your cash it's pretty hard to run after him with a guitar in your hand, or worse still leave the guitar down and believe me it won't be there when you get back.

I used to play the usual stuff, Bob Dylan, Eagles and Bruce Springsteen but I did start writing some of my own stuff, my situation at home had changed.
I vividly remember it I was sitting in the living room, my back to the rear garden, Dawn my wife of 4 years walked into the room, stood in front of me and said "Do you want a divorce".
I looked up from my newspaper shrugged my shoulders and said "ok" and within a few months I was divorced and out of my house.

Before I go on any further I do want to say Dawn was a lovely wonderful person, I think I married too soon, we remained friends and I'm glad to say there was no spitting or hatred.

I moved out and bought my own house, it was different though I was on my own, my brother had moved to the states about 8 years earlier, my mother and father had sold up and moved back to Ireland so I found myself very much alone.

I had a few friends, not many but I used to keep my curtains drawn and not answer the doorbell if it rang, I never really thought about it until I started writing this but I probably had a touch of depression, something I know a bit more about since my stroke.
So with the curtains drawn and myself withdrawn my salvation was my guitar, I would spend hours and hours trying to master its intricacies, eventually managing to knock out a few tunes, any other musician reading this will understand how painful your fingers become when you start learning, even to the point of bleeding, it takes about a year to really harden the tips of your fingers to the point where you can play for hour after hour.

After learning a few songs, I started experimenting with writing my own, now everyone has a different system and there is no right way or wrong way, Bernie Taupin would write the lyrics give them to Elton John and he would compose the music, my method was to come up with a melody then write the words around it…. Worked for Ozzy Osbourne.
To be honest the first few songs I wrote where not only crap but also quite depressing, I suppose it's much easier to write about dark and depressing times than happy go lucky occasions but it gave me a focus and without it and my guitar I think I would have spiralled downwards.

It was this time that I met my second wife Karen, we had known each other since we had been kids, I was friends with her older brother when we met, I think we were both at a vulnerable time in our lives, she had split from a long term relationship and me just divorced.

Karen's chap was not a very nice guy and when I mentioned Ireland and a visit to see my folks Karen got very excited asking if we might move there on a permanent basis, her life in Birmingham wasn't the easiest and she looked at it as a second chance.
On a visit over to see my folks my dad spotted an advert for a Clerk of Works for the Dublin Corporation, a clerk of works was somebody on a construction site who represented the client and ensured all works complied with the specification and all codes of practise. They would interact with the building surveyor, Architect or Engineer on issues of quality, instructions required and record keeping.
The job title is believed to derive from the 13th century when monks and priests (i.e. "clerics" or "clerks") were accepted as being more literate (Ha, that's me) than the builders of the age and took on the responsibility of supervising the works associated with the erection of churches and other religious property.

After spending a month with mom and dad, I was asked to attend an interview in Dublin and it coincided with my return to England, so I went for the interview and then caught the boat back home, and a few weeks later I got a letter offering me the job.

I got in touch with a letting agency and soon my house was rented out and I was on my way across the water to Ireland in search of fame and fortune…. Oh strike that last bit, I was just going to start a new job.
At age 32, I turned up at my Mom and Dad's house with black bin bags full of clothes an electric can opener, my TV and a VCR, for all you younger folk, a VCR is an old fashioned DVD player.

32 years old and all my belongings fitted into the back seat of my car and I still had room to pick up a hitch hiker if I wanted to.

I will never forget the Ferry crossing that night, it was late October 1992, I had been on some rough crossings but none like this, I was never normally nervous but whilst holding on to a rail as I tried to move about I came on one of the crew members, he looked straight at me, "We shouldn't be out here" he said, "all other vessels were confined to port, there are no other ships out here, we are on our own," he looked pretty scared and after hearing that my bum cheeks were vibrating quicker than a grasshoppers knees .
All the goods in the shops were tumbling around on the floor, suddenly there was a bang and a trolley full of dishes burst through the kitchen door, travelled about 20m and crashed into a table, crockery flying everywhere, the tables and some of the chairs were bolted to the floor but the loose chairs were tumbling around you needed to be very careful.
Then there was an almighty crash as the boat smacked down after been pushed up by a wave and the TV and I'm not talking about a tiny flat screen, I'm on about the old traditional TV, 28-inch screen and weighed in at about 100kg's crashed onto the floor, it would have killed someone had they been sitting under it.

Eventually calmness prevailed and we docked in Dublin port, North wall, the announcement came over the tanoy for drivers to go down to their vehicles, on reaching my own car I found my own TV had slipped of the front seat and wedged itself in the foot well, as we drove off I passed a number of waggons that had toppled over and were resting on the side of the vessel

42

CH. 4

27ᵗʰ May- The death of my first life, the beginning of my second

None of us can remember been born and maybe that's a good thing, I mean the occasion is very special but in reality it's all a bit messy.

Unfortunately for me I do remember the beginning of life part 2.

It was a Monday morning, 27ᵗʰ May 2013, Claire's alarm went off and although I didn't have to get up as early as her I was awoken by her morning chorus of yawns etc.
I leaned over, arm stretched out waiting to feel the familiar touch of my IPad, I powered up and started to catch up on news of the day. What newspaper App? I hear you ask, no not a newspaper, that was full of depressing boring news.
No, I wanted the real news, the gossip so I of course was on Facebook.
My finger pulling the page as I gave each person 4 words to warrant my attention before spinning past their post, in the back ground I would have the radio playing away, now and again my finger halting the page as I either took interest on someone else's post or an item they had shared, it could be anything from dogs that could surf to pranksters terrifying their roommates.
By this time Claire had already left for work, time for me to get up, I turned over to put my pad back on the locker and got a sudden feeling of pins and needles in my arm, at first I just thought it was

the way I had been lying but in a millisecond I just knew, don't ask me how but I knew, I was in trouble.

I reached out with my right arm for my phone, I found it, looked at it as I unlocked it and just said to myself "DO IT"

I dialled 999, the number you never want to dial, a voice answered.
"Emergency services which service do you require?"
"Ambulance please"
"What's the nature of your emergency"
I told her, I think I'm having a stroke but instead of some soothing reassuring words, she said
"How on earth do you know you're having a stroke"

In my head I remembered that TV advert F.A.S.T.
F – face and the left side of my face was getting numb
A - arm, I was losing feeling in my arm
S – Speech, I was still able to talk but I did slur some of my words
T -time to call help.
I started to tell the girl my symptoms, I was still talking when she cut across me, "please give me your address caller an ambulance has been dispatched,
I gave directions, I could hear her talking to the ambulance control centre.
"Do you want to stay on the line caller"
"No not at all", I said, I felt embarrassed like I wasn't a real emergency, I mean I was very calm, it didn't make sense, why wasn't I screaming out for help?

I decided I had better get up and unlock the front door, it seemed the right thing to do, I stood up went to take a step, my next

memory is of a girl in green kneeling over me saying "Jon, can you hear me", she repeated it several times, I tried to answer her but the words wouldn't come out, then all of a sudden I spoke, but it was all slurred I couldn't do it, I tried again, I still slurred but I managed to say "yes".
I don't remember the next while so I shall tell it as Claire told me.

She came home to find not one but two ambulances at the house, my mother who was in the Granny flat heard the ambulances, she had come out side but they wouldn't let her in to me, they just kept telling her everything would be ok. She was the one who called Claire telling her its ok that I had just fallen.

Claire got to the bedroom, I was on the floor, the bed had been moved over tight to the wall to give access, thank god I still had a T-shirt and underwear on to save my blushes.
There was a discussion going on regarding my weight, they had obviously attended the 'Safe Handling courses', now I know I am a big chap but Claire told me their guess's where way over and what was my weight? well you'll have to marry me to know that and I already have a wife, actually when this happened we weren't married, but that's another chapter.

So I was put into the ambulance and Claire travelled with me, apparently the oxygen mask was pissing me off and I had a constant battle with the paramedic, me pulling the mask off and she refitting it, I was also talking crap and mumbling away.

I was taken to University College Hospital Galway (UCHG)
I had a conversation with Claire about 3 months after my stroke,

Claire wanted to see how much I remembered about my time in UCHG as we were chatting, I said, "I think I was dreaming, I heard a voice saying 'He's not a well man, the next 72 hrs. will be critical, if he survives that then he may have a chance,' "I felt very afraid and alone, but then I dreamt the same voice saying 'Jon is as well as we could hope, he's past the 72 hrs., his chances of survival are much improved', I felt relief and not as scared".
As I was telling this to Claire the colour drained from her face, she said "That was what the consultant had said to her, you were unconscious, we didn't think you could hear us".

Claire refused to leave my bedside despite the hospital staff telling her to go home, she was sleeping on the chair when one of the nurses taking pity on her gave her some large cushions which Claire placed on the floor and slept beside me
This went on for a number of days then one day I opened my eyes and spoke, it was all mumbled rubbish, I was on about having to get into work.
Claire was feeding me soup and something that was more like baby food, all of my left side was affected which includes my throat and therefore my swallow.

I have some small vague memories of my time in UCHG, my most prominent one, was me, continuously asking Claire for a sausage sandwich, I was not really supposed to have major solids but- hey ho, she is a nurse.
All this time I never really thought seriously about what had happened to me, I think it's like a survival mechanism embedded in my damaged broken brain, stopping me from worrying or going into depression, at least for a while anyway.
I do have one lasting memory and that is the kindness and patience

the nursing staff had with me. Angels is what they call them and Angels they are, I made sure I went back about a year later to say thank you to them and I will give them a 6.437% discount on my book. (only joking)

I found that using Facebook (FB) as a diary I could record what was happening whilst keeping in touch with friends, below are some excerpts.

June 6th
FB. Can I just say a big thank you for all the wonderful messages I received and to all who have taken the time to call in and visit, it has meant so much and helps me keep positive, I don't think of myself as a stroke victim but as a stroke survivor and I will make a full recovery my incentive is my life with Claire I want to be her companion not her patient hope to see yee all soon

June 7th
FB .I am not able to go to work at this moment in time thought I would give public service thoughts on a daily basis and to days thought is on Irish morning TV, I have heard some people refer to it as been shite, well I totally disagree I think early morning Irish tv is really really shite in fact it is the pits and nothing short of a fecking disgrace . So, there you have it, so tune in tomorrow for my thoughts on the Irish banks.

JUNE 8th
FB. Apparently, a big bunch of fecking eejits had a meeting in Europe and have decided that when a bank goes tits up that major investors who have made billions from there guaranteed

investments should help bail the bank out when the drain of their profits put the bank into negative equity and not take money from the ordinary Joe soap and ask him to bail the bank OUT.

Now they are patting themselves on the back for what they consider a brilliant bit of policy making on their behalf, these geniuses are known as euro MP's I prefer to call them money grabbing bastards. I mean it's not rocket science, if a bank goes tits up let the investors pay not the public.... Is it a coincidence that bankers rhymes with wankers I think not? Tune in for tomorrow's thought. Bye bye for now.
Please excuse my spelling not feeling too good.

I remember been told that they were moving me to Merlin Hospital, I was still very confused, I did not really understand the extent of my injuries for a good few weeks, so off I went just a short journey to unit 4, this was the stroke unit, I ended up in room on my own it was a single room, oh how it felt like heaven a nice quite single room all to myself, happy to take the solitude this small island of solace gave me.

Claire realising my nervousness stayed again by my side sleeping on a chair, I would wake up in the middle of the night in a confused state of panic, and she would help calm me down, I think I had reached that stage where I started to understand the extent of my injuries

   There was a bell so we could call a nurse, but mine was not plugged in, they were not too keen on doing that as they did not like to be disturbed, now just to qualify, that was not the case with all the staff, just a few, Claire had gone home and I woke in the early hours of the morning to find I had partially slipped into the frame on the side of my bed, the frame that stops you falling out of bed, my leg and arm were wedged in it and I could not move, I called out for what seemed hours but I was the furthest away from the nurses station and my cries could not be heard, then eventually Claire came in to find me stuck.

She went ballistic, she shouted down the corridor for assistance and one of the nurse's aid's came down the corridor shouting "Who's making all this noise," then she entered the room and on seeing my position said "Oh my god" reaching up above my bed she rang the call bell, at the same time this lady was getting an earful from Claire including a request to make an official complaint, the nursing staff are supposed to do hourly rounds to check on the patients but we figure I was as least 3 hours in this position.

Another time I was taken to use the bathroom, using the hoist I was lifted out of bed, taken down the corridor to the bathroom, when we got there it was in use so they took me to another bathroom, shorts and underwear were pulled down and they rolled me into the cubicle or at least they tried because the hoist would not fit, after pushing and shoving what was a lost cause the two nurses wheeled me back out, heading down to the other bathroom, along a public corridor, my shorts and underwear still around my ankles and my modesty on full display, I just cried my eyes out.

The summer was by now in full swing and I had a full bank of windows along one of the walls offering me unimpeded views of the Garden around the unit.

Merlin unlike other hospitals consists of satellite building units dotted around a 100 acre grassed and tree lined expanse.

I could sit in my bed watching people stroll around the grounds enjoying the although seasonal weather it was much warmer than previous years, sometimes my heart would suddenly race as I would spot one or both of my dogs running past the window, which meant Claire was around.

The feeling was the best tonic I could ask for, my eyes would widen then Claire would come into view with the dogs running around her, it gave me my first taste of normality despite been stuck in my bed, for a few seconds everything seemed ok with the world.

The visits from Claire where regular as her own office was just around the corner, my over active mind was able to transport me outside but reality would soon kick back in and the physio's would arrive into my room and the process of getting out of bed would begin.

It was a system of straps and hoists, the whole left side of my body was a complete dead weight, all dignity was thrown out the window and as you can imagine with a major hospital there were a number of different nurses and nurse's aides who would get you out of the bed, I quickly developed my list of favourites it's not than any of the others were bad it's just that you have to understand your dignity is taken from you, there is no place for shyness or bashfulness.

It seemed that some of them came into your room picked up your dignity and placed it in a nice blanket lined box, whilst others though not discarding it, threw it over in the corner where you could pick it up later and dust it down.

I just want to put this in writing, overall the Galway nursing staff were excellent, I was living in my own world, trying to come to terms with what had happened, we forget that they to have their own lives and it can't be easy coming into work every day all smiles and cheery

After been lifted out of the bed on a hoist, I would be put into a wheel chair and taken into the physio room here there was no favours, if they said it, you had to do it, it was rightly so, I was not going to get better lying in bed although saying that the first physio sessions were conducted on a physio's bed.

They would lie me down and manipulate my leg in all sorts of direction, testing me to see what type of resistance I could put up to them.

On one of the days Claire's brother Jim was in visiting me, he had a letter in his pocket, he took it out and read it to Claire, it was about a hip replacement operation he'd been waiting for, he was to attend

Unit 1, sometime in June, in Merlin, "Where the f#cks Unit 1?" Jim asked Claire, "It's not far from here, I'll show you" said Claire.

As it happened it was just a few hundred metres down from unit 4, a few days later Claire was wheeling me across the road heading to unit 1 to visit Jim, it all seemed a bit surreal that I was getting out of my hospital bed to go and visit Jim.

We get to the ward and surprise surprise, even before we open the door we can hear Jim's voice as he's holding court in the ward.

He's that kind of person, never known as a shy man sitting quietly in the corner.

We entered and there was Jim sitting up in bed fixing a neighbouring patients glasses, laughing away with the other patients. He's one of these characters that within 5 minutes of meeting him he will either know someone you know or has been to the same village where you live.

He went up to our Donegal cottage one weekend, the next time we went up no matter who we met they all said "How's Jim" …. He knew more people after one visit than Claire and I knew after 12 months

It is quite amazing how methods have changed in hospitals, one time you had an operation and it was all about rest and recuperation, Jim had his operation and the next morning they had him up taking his first steps then 2 days later discharged and away home.

17th June- I suppose you're wondering why I have the date in bold letters, well I'll tell ya, it's my birthday, I couldn't believe I was still in hospital on my birthday, I never mentioned it to the staff but your date of birth is a very visible item, it's on your medical sheet on your wrist band etc. So I got birthday wishes from them, I tried to luck excited but I just wanted to go home, maybe wake up and find out it was just a real shitty dream.

The day was quite warm and sunny, Claire came in with a card as did her sister Cathy, Cath also had a lovely homemade cake from one of her friends.
We took it down to the TV room and Cath started to slice the cake up. There was another patient in there, now just to say when I talk of other patients I will change their names, so let's call him Pat, pat was in his late 60's early 70's and Cathy asked if he'd like a slice of cake, a big grin and a nod followed and Cath gave him what could only be deemed a fair decent slice, a few minutes later, Cathy noticed a tag on Pat that said *'no solids'*, you see a lot of stroke victims struggle with their swallow as the muscles on one side of the throat don't work, so Claire and Cathy suddenly rose to their feet dashed over to Pat in order to separate him from the cake, but this old boy had other ideas and considering his age he started throwing shapes that Brian O Driscoll would have been proud of, at the same time eating as much cake as he could,
Now Cath and Claire are both nurses and they ceased their action saying "Oh just let him enjoy it, there's enough of us here to keep an eye on him," oh I forgot Cath's husband, Ray was there, and he's another nurse, so the pursuit finished and poor old pat was left to savour the rest of his cake, washed down with a good strong cup

of tea.

We left the TV room and wandered outside, Claire had parked her car under some trees giving shade from the unusually hot Irish summer day. We tailgated for a while then we got word back from the Ward Sister that I could be let off the hospital grounds so a Taxi was called and soon we were heading to Salthill (The sea side area of Galway).

I was nervous as the taxi driver pushed me up into the back of the adapted van, but soon we had left the hospital grounds I was tasting freedom; I remember I had my arm out of the sliding window beside me it just felt brilliant…. normal.

We soon reached the sea side and I commenced my first outing as a disabled man, I very quickly noticed you get extremes, either someone who just thought I was a nuisance and wouldn't move to let my wheelchair pass or those that made an exaggerated move to get out of my way.
I could feel a lot of eyes looking at me, all of a sudden my delight at been outside started to change, to make things worse some of the paths were nearly impossible to traverse, and there was a bit of pulling and dragging to keep me moving, of course I had travelled the same section of road many time over the last 20 years or more but you never think that one day you'll end up in a wheelchair.
We got a take away and sat at an outdoor table watching the world go by.
Someone gave me a bottle of non-alcoholic beers and I slurped at it whilst enjoying the take out, I don't know if this was a trick of the brain but I gave the bottle to Claire, my head felt woozy

My day was starting to change, I felt uncomfortable, I can't believe I was thinking it but I just wanted to go back to what had now become my comfort zone… My hospital bed.

The Taxi was summoned and eventually it turned up again a van but not the same one, the driver pulled out the ramp not like the other one this time it was a single ramp, he started to push me up, Claire wasn't happy she screamed at him to stop, one of my wheels went off the edge I grabbed on to my chair with my good hand all I could hear was Claire screaming at the driver to get me down, slowly I was brought back down to Tera firma.

I looked around, a small gathering of onlookers had stopped to see what was going on, I'm not a small bloke but that day I just shrank into my chair trying to make myself as small as possible.

Eventually another taxi arrived and I was soon back in the hospital and into the comfort of my own bed.

JUNE18th

I started working with the physios from a seated and sometimes standing position, mainly reaching to my right side but extending through my effected left side.

It was repetitive work but it had to be done, the brain even after it has been damaged, pathways will try and reroute messages to the body, it's a bit like a road diversion, the usual route is closed for say a river flood that has taken the road out, so an alternative route is found and the traffic can flow, this means a lot of the physio work is pure repetition. In effect you are trying to retrain the brain

I did start to see some small improvements, then one Sunday evening whilst in the bed I moved my left leg up i.e. bending at the knee, Claire said "Do you know you just did that, I mean is that what you tried to do" and I said "yea, I think so", I moved my knee down then lifted it up again, Clare jumped up and started clapping, it was my first sign of controlled movement in four weeks, then the Friday came.

I had been for an MRI scan that morning, When I first entered the hospital they gave me a CAT scan it showed my bleed, but there was a lot of blood blocking the view of the brain, I needed the MRI, a more detailed scan for the doctors, not a nice thing, you have to lie perfectly still for 20 – 25 mins whilst in the machine which is also very noisy as it scans my brain as it was a requirement to check the blood had gone, i.e. Had been absorbed, the results came back and that was the case, the blood was gone and no other bleeding visible, so thumbs up all around.
I was taken back to my ward, very stiff and also still pumped up from the whole event.
Next thing the physio's where down to my room, I didn't feel in form to go but I went anyway, the session wasn't too long and towards the end they were getting me to rise from a seated position to a stand, but then as I returned to sit they had me stop and hold it a couple of inches before reaching the seat.

Then it happened, bang, a shooting pain to the back of my head, tingling to the left side of my face, symptoms that seemed oh so familiar, another stroke, I yelled out and collapsed onto the physio's bench, it was familiar yet so unfamiliar as the pain in the back of my head was like a hot poker, I never had pain when my stroke occurred, but the tingling up my neck and behind my ear, I did have that before, I screamed out, the physio's gathered around me, they were shouting my name, I remember just saying "it hurts" through a grimacing face, one of the physio's said "get him back to the ward quickly".

I was wheeled back into my room, I felt exhausted then everyone left, the pain had subsided a bit but I was shaking like a leaf, I was scared, really scared I reached out to my locker and picked up my phone I was totally convinced I was going to die, I just wanted to hear Claire's voice, I wanted to say goodbye but how do you do that, I called her number but it went straight to message minder, in a split second my conscience kicked in, 'do not be the world's biggest bastard and leave a goodbye message on her phone, that's just not fair'

So I just said 'hello, call me when you can' then I pushed the red button and hung up.

I was in my wheelchair just staring at the ground tears falling from my eyes then with a startle I realised my phone was ringing, it was Claire, I answered "Hello", then just started crying, I heard her say 'Hiya' then she just shouted Jon, Jon what's wrong? I just about managed to say "I think I'm having another stroke" and the phone slipped from my hand on to the floor, I continued crying convinced all was at an end.

I know her office was close to the hospital but it really did seem to be just 10 seconds and she was there in the room beside me calling my name and repeating "Jon are you ok", she turned took one step to the doorway and just screamed down the corridor "Why isn't this man in his bed?" within seconds a young nurse came into the room, the young nurse and Claire lifted me from the wheelchair and got me into bed, I was still shaking with fear but did feel safer now, Claire was here.

The young nurse was in fact a student nurse called Joanne, and she punched well above her student title, she took my blood pressure, "Jon, your blood pressure is good, that's a really good sign, I don't think you're having a bleed" she said, smiled and then spoke to Claire, she came in about every 10 - 15 mins checking my BP and each time it was ok.

I started to relax down a little, a doctor came in and repeated Joanne's words.

All this time Claire was sat at my side, several hours had passed and thankfully I had not met god, just to pass the time Claire had picked up a small cardboard box that was beside my bed, it had a number of different items such as soft material, a scouring pad etc. all differing in texture to rub on my hand and arm to see if I could feel anything, so as I lay on the bed with my eyes closed Claire was rubbing the stroke side of my face very gently with one of these cloths, my eyes opened, "did you feel that" she said, "yes" I said, she sat bolt upright, "did ya," her voice changed from soft spoken to one of surprise "yes" I said again, so she spent the next hour, me with my eyes closed whilst she touched my face with varying degrees of pressure to see what my reaction would be, and it did seem I had a bit more feeling in my face, so after the horror of the day we turned it around saying maybe my brain was making new pathways and that caused my earlier pain.

Then it came time for Claire to head home, "I'll stay if you want" she said "no, no you head home get your sleep" whilst at the same time screaming in my head "please stay, don't leave me".

I didn't think I'd sleep that night but within minutes I was in a dream world.

The Doctor came into my room July 8th a few weeks after my bad turn, to discuss a date for leaving, he reckoned I could go home in a couple of weeks, it was like music to my ears, I lay back in my bed just to let the news soak in, I then picked up the phone to call

Claire.

Before Claire arrived, the Doctor came back into my room, he was looking all cool with an expensive pair of sunglasses on and the tie had been discarded, "Jon, we just got a call from The National Rehab Hospital Dublin (HRH), they are looking for you", "when" I asked, the doctor looked straight at me "this Wednesday"
I said nothing, I think I was in a bit of shock, then I looked up and said "that's great", a pat on the leg and he'd gone.

Claire basically bounced into the room, still on a high from my news of going home, "it's all changed" I said and went on to explain the move to the NRH, she was upbeat being the nurse she was looking at the bright side, I was going to a hospital which specialized in my condition, I just felt disappointed, I wasn't going home.

July 10th
FB. After suffering a stroke, you must just realise that some tasks are beyond reach, so after a lot of soul searching I have finally come to terms with the fact that I will never dance the lead role in riverdance.

CH5
A CHANGE OF VIEW

I'd had an interview for the NRH hospital some weeks back, they take spinal, amputees and stroke patients for intensive rehab, it was a very mixed emotion, one-minute I was going home the next I was on my way to a hospital on the other side of the country, Claire went down to the doctors room just before he left for the day, he updated her and Claire asked a load of questions I should have asked and she was so happy, it made sense, take as much treatment as I could get but as they say 'medicine can be a bitter pill'.

I collected my bits and pieces together, it was weird, most people would be delighted to be getting out of hospital but in a strange way it has become my safe place, I can't believe I'm saying this but it was where I felt comfortable.

So its Wednesday 10th July about 6.00pm I'm sitting in St Brigid's ward, lots of patients, lots of medical staff, none of them familiar to me, even the Dublin accent was so different.

Claire had made the journey up with me as I sat and looked around the unfamiliar ward, a nurse came up to us and introduced herself then pointed out my bed and my locker, I no longer had the benefits of a private room, here I was in a ward, 6 beds either side of the ward with 1 bed in what appeared to be an office, at the opposite end was the nurses station where came a continuous drone of voices which would remain so for the next 3 months, then on the other side of the nurses station was the female ward.

July 11th

FB. Today is Thursday, Claire went home to Galway last night, I have text and spoke with her this morning but if I'm honest I've checked my phone for messages just about every ten minutes, I miss her so much but I have to let her get back to some normality or I'm scared of losing her, it's all about the patients here nobody seems to think about the people doing the caring, the loved ones, but there life is changed just about as much, Claire can't make me get better it's up to me, so it's hard for her and others as they watch the person in their life struggle to rebuild a new life, but I intend to work hard and when I marry Claire I will gain a wife and not a nurse.

It was all a bit quiet at first, I met with the physio who told me they did not know I was coming in and as yet there was no programme ready for me, I was to say the least a bit disappointed as I wanted to keep the momentum from Galway going.

I did get some good news, the doc said I could go home for the weekend, Friday quickly came and we headed off but things did not really go the way I wanted.

One thing I found from the stroke was that no matter how much you plan something there will always be the unknown.

When we got back to Galway the upgrading works to the house which were due to be completed Friday where still on going so we returned to a building site, there was dust everywhere, that naturally caused tempers to be slightly on edge, I went to bed that night and although I did not say anything I was very scared, I was now back in the bed where the stroke happened, not the best way to try and get a good night's sleep.

I woke in the early hours very un-comfortable, after waiting an hour I woke Claire, understandably she was not impressed but I persuaded her to help me to the recliner, I did sleep better there but not much.

Saturday started better, we went to mass in the morning and on our return Claire started cleaning up after the builders and kitchen man.

She asked what I wanted to do, so I eventually ended up stretched out in the living room on a recliner watching TV.

I'm not sure how long I was there but I fell asleep, then I remember waking up, very confused, I had no idea where I was and no knowledge of the stroke, I started to try and get up but obviously I could not move, I could not comprehend what had happened, I started to roll and thrash about at the same time screaming out, Claire heard the commotion, she came in trying to calm me down, I still had no idea about the stroke, then just as quickly realisation began to kick in, I just started crying, inconsolably, it felt like the stroke all over again, if I'm honest it was such a low point for me.

I returned back to the hospital Sunday evening, I felt low but it was obvious that Claire was just shattered, I knew hand on heart that I had to let go some of the dependency I have on her, if not I felt there was a slight chance, not losing her but changing our relationship.

The delay in my programme meant that at least I had some time to find my feet at my new home, my ward was on the 4th floor and the most decrepit old lift served the floor (to be fair it never broke down whilst I was there) it wasn't meant for wheelchairs and over the weeks and months we learned how to get as many people and wheelchairs in as we could, I'm sure it was over the capacity rating, anyhow myself and Claire explored my new surroundings over the couple of days, the ground floor had numerous buildings but for me my life revolved around The Quadrant a 4 sided corridor with glass on the inner side that looked out onto a small garden, right in the middle of the hospital, there was a patients dining room for patients only and a second dining room that was accessible to visitors and patients.

My first evening meal I ate with Claire but she was told that the hospital preferred me to eat in the patients dining room so as to get me mixing with others.
When it came time for Claire to leave, it reminded me of a time over 40 years previous when my mother left me to walk through the school gates and although surrounded by many people I was all alone for the first time in my life, and this time I felt very alone once more.
I wheeled myself as best I could (I'll expand on that statement in a minute) into the patients dining room looking back at Claire and she never moved, standing still, just as my mother did all those years previously.

July 12TH

FB. *So, meal times in the national rehabilitation hospital can be, mmmmmm let's see, ah yes Interesting, there are a few places where one can eat but I tend to use the patients canteen it can be different.*

I have to say that some of the menus are quite strange for example the other evening they served Bacon and cabbage, good healthy Irish style meal or at least it would have been only for the lump of fat approx. the size of Scotland, attached to a minuscule piece of bacon another day I was given steak after a good twenty five minutes chasing it around the plate and in the process scattering all my vegetables onto the table I just picked it up with my good hand and ripped into it much to the disgust of some of the watching nurse's aids, but when needs must, I think putting peas on a stroke victim's dinner plate is just taking the piss........ Later folks

The wheelchair they provided me with had it been a car it would have failed its NCT, (National Car Test) To start with its not ideal to push a wheelchair with only one hand but to do it with a sticking wheel just meant all my efforts resulted in me spinning on the spot, I looked like a fat break-dancer on wheels.

Back to the ward, my life started to take on a routine, from Monday to Friday I had a pretty full time table that usually started at 8.00 to 8.30am, firstly there was the Occupational Therapist better known as the OT, my OT was Fiona a very kind lovely girl with the most beautiful Donegal accent.

The first lessons where around dressing and ablutions, now when you got up in the mornings someone would pull a cover around the bed for privacy.

This one morning one of the male attendants had just landed me back from having a shower, I was sat on the bed nothing on, busy drying myself when I heard this soft Donegal accent asking "which bed is Jon McGinley in, next thing the curtain was pulled back, in stepped Fiona and the curtain closed.

"Hello" she said "I'm Fiona" and held out her hand to shake, now you have to remember I only had one usable hand and that was tied up trying to keep the towel around me and save my blushes.

"erm" I said "can you give me a minute; I don't have any clothes on"

"That's why I'm here" she said "I can't teach you how to dress yourself one handed if your already dressed."

She looked and seen my obvious embarrassment and said "Jon I've seen hundreds of naked men; I promise I won't get embarrassed". So off came the towel and she proceeded to show me lesson 1. Putting on underpants one handed, actually that should be underwear nobody says underpants anymore but I stand to be corrected.

As silly as it may sound her methods where tried and tested and I still use them today.

july 18th

FB. Today I want to talk about my stroke, we all have had friends or relatives that have suffered a stroke but what does it really mean, ok let's jump from the day of my stroke to now some 8 weeks later, so I woke up this morning actually had a great sleep thanks to a piraton last night so when I wake there is not much I can do by means of getting ready for the day, you see to stop me falling out of bed the sides have been pulled up, I have to wait for a nurse to drop the sides, I then have to push myself with the good leg to a position where I can drop my legs over the side, then with my right hand pull myself up to a sitting position, if I'm not due a shower I wait for a bowl of water and start washing, all fairly normal until I get to my left side, I lean forward to let my left arm drop down this allows me to get under the arm making me all fresh and clean, put a bit of roll on deodorant the same way mmmmmm smelling good. Next, get the jocks and fish around for my left leg, once snared pull up a bit, in with the right leg, stand up and yank well, next lay t shirt on my knees thread my weak left arm through the sleeve, important to get sleeve over the elbow, continue with right arm over the head then pull into place, you get the idea all similar with remaining bits of clothing main difference it can now take me 20 to 25 mins to dress myself, shoes are a bit harder but am slowly getting there. So how do I get around, as I only have power in one arm when I push my wheel chair it just goes around in circles, I have to use my right leg to block the chair from turning it works although some days my leg can be badly bruised, alternatively I can use my right leg to push the chair backwards, I tend to use this option when travelling the full length of the corridors. Later peeps Claire's here.

Once a week the Consultant would do her rounds, her real name will remain in my head for the rest of my life as she was not a nice person and amongst the patients she was better known as 'Old Steel Britches' because we believed no one had ever managed to get them off.

She started her rounds continuously turning to a number of

students who followed her like a little pack of Terriers all trying to vie for the best position.
She would talk loudly about the patients, so much so that all the patients could clearly hear what she was saying.
She would ask the mandatory question "And how are you today" but before anyone could respond she would hit you with another question then turn her back to make some comment to her litter of pups.

One of the patients across from me had his stroke on the opposite side which causes loss of speech and could only swear, his name was Tony, so anyway old steel britches reaches him and he lets a big roar and just shouts "Fuck", Steel britches turns and gives him a load of South Dublin posh abuse, so Tony lets rip again and she just roared at him.
What I know about strokes could be written on a postage stamp, yet even I knew he could not help himself, I watched as the ward nurses turned away in embarrassment.
Not a nice person.

As I was telling you earlier the physio's had come up to the ward with three different wheelchairs, one I swear was for a child of about 6, one was a light weight collapsible type which they just took one look at me then announced out loudly "No good won't take his weight" then as an afterthought they looked over at me asking "What weight are you Jon," to which I replied "Too heavy for that one apparently", and with that they seemed happy…. so the last option was an early 16th century model and guess which one I got, yes of course I ended up with Shackleton, that's what I named it after Ernest Shackleton the polar explorer whose equipment although fine for its time, it was antiquated and not fit for purpose.

So, now I had the chance to bring it to the attention of Steel britches,
She reached my bed took up my notes "And this is erm erm
Jon McGinley" then turned to her Terriers and started to give them the history of my stroke whilst her Terriers jostled in front of her.
"How are you settling in Mr McGinley"….. Ahh at last here it was the chance I'd been waiting for "Fine thank you but I'm having a problem with my wheel chair" the words had only just had the chance to leave my mouth when all of a sudden the flat palm of her hand was right in front of my face like a traffic warden on heat.
"Medical matters only Mr McGinley, medical matters only"
"Well it is a medical matter" I said
"No it isn't Mr McGinley"
"Sorry" I said "but I think it is, as my wheelchair can only go around in circles I keep getting dizzy"

Now I know it…. My friends know it…. My family know it, YES I HAVE A SMART GOB and although has got me out of sticky situations it has got me in to plenty of trouble and if I'm honest, probably didn't help in my relationship with Steel Britches, I'm sure we'll hear more from her.

The Galway Hospice had been brilliant to Claire and she stayed with me in Dublin as long as she could, but eventually she had to go, and more to the point I had to let her go.
I remember as she walked out of the ward although I could not see it, I could hear the ping of the lift as it arrived…. Then she was

gone.

I got into my chair and wheeled myself backwards as this was the only way I could make the chair go in a straight line, got to the lift went down to the front entrance, sat in my chair staring out the door to the carpark, just in the faint hope that Claire might come back, maybe she forgot her keys or her purse, just anything that might bring her back, the wind was blowing the rain in the front door as well as getting cold I was getting wet, I didn't care, then all of a sudden a voice beside just said, "you all right mate," I was woken from my carpark stare and a young guy in his 30's was in front of me in a wheel chair with a false leg sticking up in the air, it took me a couple of seconds to figure out what I was looking at, "yeah thanks I'm fine" "come on" he said you'll catch yer death sitting there, then they'll have to take you to a proper hospital,"
I started to wheel around using my one good leg to push me backwards whilst transfixed by this false leg sticking up from between his legs.
Whilst waiting for the lift my big gob clicked into gear and it came out "wouldn't it be easier to wear the leg instead of carrying it"
"Oh he smiled it's a new one and it's not run in yet"
I looked over trying not to laugh but couldn't help it I burst out laughing it was then that I realised it was ok, we could laugh at ourselves, we could pull the piss out of each other, it helped us to cope.
I have the most wonderful memory of sitting in my wheelchair at the doorway to the dining room some 5 minutes before it opened and hearing a number of voices shouting and laughing, then from around the corner came a wheelchair been pushed by a patient in another wheelchair, been pushed by another etc.
All in all, there was a line of 8 wheelchairs with each occupant

pushing the chair in front and at the very end was a lad with only one leg pushing the whole sharabang laughing his head off, they roared past us screaming and shouting to cheers and applause from the rest of us, and completed a lap of the quadrangle before finishing at the dining hall and unsurprisingly a roar of fucks from those with bruised and grazed knuckles.

It's amazing as I write this, a story about the lowest time in my life and yet as I read back on the notes and diaries I kept I find myself chuckling away at my desk.

Aug 5th
FB. So it's been a few days since my last confession, it's been a mixed few days still no movement in the hand but some seriously bad pain in the shoulder, I suppose on a scale of 1 to 10 it's about a 6 which I can take but after 5 hours 8 hours etc. it just becomes unbearable and complete agony, I cried a lot Friday from the pain and would have gladly cut my arm off if it stopped the pain, so the journey home for the long weekend did not start well. The pain is nerve pain so no amount of stretches helps.

So with Friday over and the pain diminishing I went to bed and fell asleep and what a night I had I woke at about 2 am. and at first felt great and happy with my sleep, then as I shut the eyes to try and drop off again I got a strong smell, I tried to ignore it but as I inhaled through my nose it was there again except this time more intense, I called Claire she woke, "what's up" she asked only just waking from her sleep, some things wrong I said "what is it?" she asked at the same time getting up and switching on the light then a quick scream of exclamation as it became apparent the bedside locker was smoking and close to flames, you see a small spot light I was using to give me some light if I woke during the night had rolled against the locker causing the heat build-up, what can I say we were so lucky, it burnt two holes in the locker, completely my fault and I have to say I shivered when I thought of what the outcome could have been.

AUG7th
FB. Today seemed to be going well the weather was good much like my mood, then about 8.30 this evening it changed, I decided to go to the loo, not that I was desperate but more just something to do, my mistake. I was getting up out of wheel chair, caught my foot on the foot plate and went down, I was on the toilet floor for about 30 mins trying to get up before I was spotted, could have been much worse but am scared in case they take my stick away, will find out tomorrow.

Aug 8th
FB. So last night was not good after my fall, I spent most of the night thinking how I would have done things different so very little sleep also they moved my bed down the ward which pleased me but the right side of the bed was next to a partition which meant I could not reach my water bottle because it was now to my left, my stroke side, I didn't want to call the nurses as they don't like to be disturbed which made for a bad night but today was better and as I write this Claire is less than an hour away, I can't wait to see her, talk later guys good luck.

Aug 14th
FB. Today is a good day as I had my first breakfast in the canteen instead of on the ward I know my life will never be the same but when I see some of the folk up here I realise how lucky I am, some cannot talk or communicate or mix with others for example, we all have hospital wrist bands but one lad on my ward, no names for

obvious reasons, is very mobile and has full use of his limbs, but he has a second wrist bands that stop the doors from opening as he would just disappear and would not be aware of his surroundings so I am lucky, no not lucky, that's the wrong word, I am more fortunate than some and need to remember that, talk to ya soon, thanks for messages of support.

You never think of the devices that can help you until you need them, a swivel pad to help get in and out of a car, a knork for one handed people, it's a fork with one side sharpened so it can cut through meat and potatoes etc. I remember seeing a device in the OT room one day, it was a sort of small frame sitting on a table while I waited to see Fiona, my usual pondering mind looked trying to figure what it was, it was only many weeks later when I saw a young girl practising with it in the ladies ward as I passed on my way to the lift, it was a frame that allowed a lady to put on her bra one handed, just to point out she was practising over her T-shirt but I just thought what a brilliant bit of independence kit.
To think of all the hundreds of men out there not capable of getting a bra off with 2 good hands and there sat this girl putting it on and off with 1 hand, god bless her I hope she's doing fine today.

My physio wasn't going as well as I hoped, the therapist I had didn't always see things the same way as me, I suppose I was in a hurry I wanted more and more physio but as the hospital I was in was the only one of its type in the country, they were under pressure, but this meant I was only getting physio 3 times a week, 4 times if I was lucky, I remember one Monday I had travelled up for 9.00am got to my bed where I would find my new timetable for the week, this particular week I arrived to find I had no physio until Wednesday, I was really pissed off, so later that same day I was down on the ground floor quadrangle where at one end of the square there where some bars, a bit like parallel bars and I started walking up and down using the bars, I'd been at it for about 20 minutes when out from one of the rooms stepped my physio, our eyes met, his face locked in that position that just says distain, he moved his hand in a dismissive manner and walked past me.

Now I was in no position to go chasing him so I just had to make my way back to my wheelchair using the hand rails.

I wheeled myself as fast as I could up to the physio's ward as I looked through the glass I could see Derek working with another patient so I sat just inside the doors waiting for my opportunity, a couple of times Derek looked up but no acknowledgement, he finished with the patient it was lunch time all the other physio's where passing me as they headed for lunch but Derek went to his office, I slipped out of the physio's room but waited just outside the door keeping an eye on his office through one of the small glass panels, eventually he walked out of his office, I became the Lion in the long grass, remaining perfectly still, not even blinking as I watched my prey getting ever closer, at last the door opened Derek suddenly spotted me, a small look of surprise appeared on his face but in a microsecond it changed back to the one of distain, he went to walk past me "Derek" I shouted he stopped briefly but then continued on "Oh Derek" getting louder "wait there, I've just waited 20 minutes for you to finish, you can at least have the decency to acknowledge me"

"Jon, what is it you want", he eventually said

"I want to know what that was about outside when you saw me working on the bars" I replied.

Derek stopped turned to face me

"I don't think I want to work with you, you're not prepared to do as I

say"
He went to turn away again, my blood was boiling and it just came out "Who the fuck do you think you are, you don't get to play god, I'm not up here on some business course, I'm here because I had a fuckin stroke, yet when I drive across the country to get here I find nothing on my rota for 2 days. I'm just supposed to sit and wait for you to give me permission to get fuckin better……. You pompous arrogant prick".

I was breathing heavy staring straight at Derek, he hadn't moved not even flinched.
"You really have no idea…Derek, I went to bed one night a normal person and woke up a cripple, my whole life altered, every dream I had shattered, I have to look at the faces of my parents and see the hurt and pity in their eyes, yet tell them every day, Its ok, I'm doing fine"

To be fair Derek listened then we parted with none of us speaking I had nothing on my timetable for the rest of the day and after my blow out with Derek I wasn't feeling in a sociable mood, so I just went to my bed and got one of the nurses to draw the curtains around me.
I cried myself to sleep only to be woken a few hours later by Derek who was standing next to my bed repeating my name, I looked up "Derek, what can I do for you," "Here" he said, holding a walking stick towards me, I threw the bedclothes back and started twisting to get out of the bed, soon I was sitting on the bed looking at Derek, still holding the stick in front of himself, "I'm not going to ask, what that's for but What's that for?"
"It's for you, it's to be used on the ward to start with, then when you feel ready you can use it to go further afield"

As I said earlier myself and Derek had a few rows but we never fell out

I took the stick, all of a sudden the memory of my father giving me the keys to my first car came flooding back and the same word hit me INDEPENDENCE, it was just a small bit more reclaimed in this battle

I looked at Derek and just said "Cheers bud".

Aug 16th
FB. Ok so what's happening, well I've had my walking stick a few days now and have been practising, when the physio gave it to me it was on the agreement that I only walk from the bed to the chair with nursing supervision well I hope to god he's not got access to my FB page because I've been taking walks around the second floor, now before everyone thinks are sure that's great McGinley's up and walking again the steps are very small and as yet not secure when I look in a mirror as I walk I look just like a stroke victim which funnily enough is exactly what I am, but I have a plan and just like Baldrick is a very cunning plan within the next six months I mean to improve my walk to the point where a stranger would look at me and not realise my injury.

CH 6
Settling in

My life was now completely shaped around my time in the NRH, it was like day 4 of your fortnights holiday in Spain and you'd really got to know where everything was.

It wasn't unusual to gain a new neighbour as people either moved to another ward or left, for the first month I was the last bed on the left hand side of the ward but over time I found myself moving down the ward, I didn't actually mind it as I was getting closer to the door, so in my head I considered it moving closer to getting out.

As I said people came and went then one day a lad was admitted his name was Andy, we shared the same type of humour so we got on well.
Andy was suffering from MS and had lost the power of his walk, although he had been diagnosed several years earlier this was his first prolonged spell in hospital, he had 3 young children and meeting people like this really kept my head in the right place, Andy was 15 years younger than me and had a progressive illness, life can be a bitch sometimes.

Not long after Andy arrived I had a new neighbour his name was

Bobby.

Bobby had been in the National Rehab Hospital some three years previous due to head injuries he suffered after been hit by a car, he had made a remarkable recovery and was doing well, until one day he was getting some air, having a walk in the park, some local kids came up and started to taunt Bobby, they did so because they knew the more Bobby got upset, the more he stuttered.

He turned and roared at them to f**k off, the kids just continued to laugh at him so in anger he picked up a stone and threw it at them, catching one of the boys on the side of his face, Bobby doesn't remember anything after that until he woke in Beaumont hospital 3 weeks later in the Intensive Care unit, he spent a further 7 weeks in the hospital then got transferred and was now my new neighbour.

I didn't see him for the first day, the curtains remained fixed around his bed but I did hear him.
You see every new admission has bloods taken and Bobby had a fear of needles, the bloods man or Dracula as we called him…. (I know, it's not very imaginative) called up to the ward, he went inside the curtains all I heard was Bobby screaming at the top of his voice "Get that fuckin needle away from me", within a second Dracula was back outside the curtain looking a bit on the pale side.

This went on for three days, Dracula would walk up the corridor towards our ward, but unfortunately the trolley he was pushing had a squeaky wheel giving Bobby plenty of warning of his imminent arrival, Bobby, still enclosed with the curtains would just roar his expletives, the trolley would stop, the trolley would start squeaking again but getting quieter and quieter as Dracula turned and headed off.

Myself and Andy became very fond of Bobby, between the three of us we had 6 legs but Andy had no use of 2 legs, I had no use in 1 leg so with Bobby having the best of legs would be sent on errands, which he was very happy to do, such as down to the tuck shop, or lift the day's paper from an inattentive visitor. (We were in hospital, it wasn't stealing)

It was easy for Bobby to get upset, one night, all tucked up in bed I was talking to Andy via phone text, even though he was just across the ward and down a bit to the left, it was too late to be talking, the murmuring from the nurse's station was getting louder and louder, then suddenly Bobby just screamed out "Would yers shut the f**k up down there" myself and Andy were sniggering away like 2 bold school children, but Bobby went on "myself and Jon are not able to sleep with all that racket", I sat up, mortified at been brought into this rant, Andy on the other hand was still in hysterics.
"Bobby" I cried out "Yes Jon" he replied, "Now that was rude Bobby, go down there and apologise   to the girls"
There was a moments silence, then I heard the curtain as it was pulled back, Bobby heading down to the nurse's station, hands down by his side and head pointed down at the floor he said his piece, turned and headed back to bed, "Good night Jon" he said, "Night night Bobby".

I was down in the quadrangle on this particular day, heading towards the shop, I pulled up outside in my chair, then surveyed the front so as to plan my route in and passage way to pick up a biscuit and a drink, just as I was about to begin my assault a voice behind me timidly shouted help, I turned to see two girls in wheelchairs one was starting to turn blue as the other girl was trying to slap her back in an attempt to dislodge something stuck in her throat.

I turned wheeled into the shop and cried out "EMERGENCY, NURSE NEEDED, NOW, there was a coffee dock in the shop, full of nurses, their heads turned in unison looking at me, "NOW" I repeated, all of a sudden about six nurses rushed past me out into the corridor reaching the poor girl who was in trouble, one nurse pulled her head forward and a big slap to her back and eureka, success, the offending piece of sandwich flew out and the girl just sucked air in, filling her lungs, she was coughing and crying at the same time but at least she was ok.
A couple of nurses wheeled her away taking her up to her ward, the others slipped back to their seats and continued their lunchtime conversation as if nothing had happened.
I turned and spotted the other girl, she was shaking and seemed very alone, although the passageway had become very busy with onlookers wondering what all the commotion was about, so I wheeled over.

"You ok," I said
"I think so" she said, still trembling, she introduced herself, "I'm Jenny, thanks for your help, I just got into a panic."
"that's ok Jenn, it was a bit of a shock", I smiled as she looked back.

I was about to turn away and head off when Jenny asked, "will you just stay for a few minutes; I'm still shaking"

"Sure" I said, "my name is Jon", "oh, my names Jenny," she replied

"I know, you already told me"

She laughed, apologetically saying "sorry……that just happened so quickly," raising her hand up to a level position to see it shaking like a leaf.

So on went the small talk, I told Jenny about my stroke whilst, she explained how she was in a car accident, she was the back seat passenger and had no belt on, the car spun a few times, when she came around she was outside the car unable to move, to cut a long story short, she had broken her back and was completely paralysed from the waist down.

She didn't think much of my wheels, as I admired her sleek design and yes I'm talking about her wheelchair.

We chatted about family etc., she was married 3 kids and lived in Phibsborough, Dublin.

Then all of a sudden she just looked at me and said "what about sex", well that completely threw me, I turned away for a second in embarrassment, when I looked back she was just smiling then without battering an eyelid said, "Have you and your girl tried it since your stroke" "Oh," I said, ok now it makes a bit more sense, I remember my mouth moved but nothing came out, "we did" she said and went on to explain how her house had 5 steep steps going up to it and it was difficult to get home, but her family had clubbed together and paid for a nice hotel room for a couple of nights, I can't remember her husband's name but for the ease of it we'll call him Paul.

Jenny told me "Paul was nervous, not because it was sex, I mean we have 3 kids, he was nervous of hurting me, eventually we found a position that suited us both and off he went, like a steam train and then bang…. it was all over".

Jenny looked over at me, I didn't say a word yet she knew exactly what I was thinking "Ahh didn't feel a thing, but that's ok, I mean he enjoyed it and that's what matters, it was me that broke my back not him, why should he suffer"

I started laughing a kind of nervous laugh, then Jenny joined in and our laughter increased, I reached out took her hand and just gave it a squeeze "you're something else, I hope he realises how lucky he is" we became good friends whilst we were in the hospital, I would love to know how she is getting on, I did share a few things with her but maybe I'll keep those for the second book.

For those who don't know, people from Dublin are known as jackeens, it is a nick name for a Dubliner because way back there used to be a fondness for the UK Whose flag is the Union Jack, hence Jackeens, there is a close connection between Dublin and Liverpool and the Dub accent is along the lines of a scouse accent and they have a great sense of humour.

A number of the female spinal injuries were from Dublin and one of the smoking shelters was close to a bus stop and god help any good looking young man who thought it was safe to wait for a bus, Statements such as
"Oh Darling, come and give me arse a good feel, don't worry, ya won't get in trouble cos I can't feel a feckin thing" followed by a loud chorus of dirty laughter, it was continuous to the point that grown men would walk to the next stop rather than suffer abuse.

Whilst we are at the bus stop I must tell you another story about a lad from London, Terry or as we called him Tel boy for obvious reasons, a typical cockney full of self-assurance, I suppose he was a southern version of myself quick with the gob and always

searching for the next laugh, we became friends and it became very obvious to me all was not well with Tel, I was lucky I had Claire up to see me every weekend whilst I never seen anyone visit Terry. I'd ask if the wife was coming up this week but there was always some reason as to why not, then one day I spotted him in the quadrangle and pulled up beside him, it was pretty obvious something was wrong.
"Tell boy, you ok"

"Jon, I don't think I can take anymore, I've just had enough"

"Go and see the clip boards," I said, that was the name we gave to the phycologist's "have a chat with them, talk it through"

"Tried to top myself last night" he said

"feck, what happened"

So terry looks at me, "well it was about 2.00 in the morning, I got out of bed, telling the nurse I needed the jacks, but instead of going to the toilet I slipped down stairs and went outside", you have to remember this was just an ordinary hospital not a security one. Tel continued, "I waited by the road edge and eventually a bus came along, I got up from the wheelchair and threw myself as far as I could in front of the 45A bus"

"f#ck me" I said "and then what happened?"

"The f#kin bus stopped…… the door opened then eventually the driver shouted "Are you getting on"

"And what did you say"

well I just shouted "no" …. "So what you doing" shouts the driver…" "I'm trying to kill myself", Terry replied.
At this point I bit as hard as I could into my lip trying to stifle my laughter, Terry looked at me and seen me laughing, I had to go on the offensive

"Are you pulling the piss", I said
"No, no serious Jon, I was trying to top myself but the f#cker stopped in time I'm a f#ckin disaster, I can't even f#ckin kill myself, the bastard came out picked me up and told me to wait for the next bus as he was running ten minutes late".

My laughter quickly stopped I could see Terry was serious but then me and my big mouth stepped in,

"F#ck me Tell Boy, that the worst attempt at suicide I've ever heard"
He looked up and it was inevitable even he burst out laughing.

Now I did make a mention of these people earlier, we called them the clip boards, I'm not been rude, well maybe just a bit, I'm talking about the phycologists, they always seemed to have a clipboard in front of them and seemed to act as a kind of shield, what I mean by that is that as they sat in their chair the clip board was between me and them, it would move up to cover their mouths as they spoke to each other, if they are reading this can I just say I'm not trying to be rude but you are a strange breed, they would ask a question, then you'd hear "mmmm" then the head would disappear under the clip board and you would hear that slight noise a pen makes as it

moves across a page.
They would show you those black and white pictures, the one that look like an ink blot that's been folded in half.
They would start off "so Jon what do you see here" and I would look and give a genuine answer, "it's a bird".
The clip board would move back and a note would be written.

I'd do this for 5 or 6 pictures then throw one in for the craic

"so Jon, what about this one", *it looked like a horse*,
"A plane" says I, you knew what would happen next, the head would go down and lots of scribbling on the page.

Eventually one day, I asked to see what they were writing, I was refused access.
They are probably lovely family people but I did not like the clip boards.
It got to the last 2 nights in the NRH, I tried sleeping but it just wasn't going to happen, I don't know if it was a deliberate action but as my time in the NRH was coming to an end my bed kept getting moved down the ward, getting closer to the door which meant every time someone came in the corridor lights would shine in on top of me, maybe there was method in their madness, this spot in the ward was not conducive with somebody needing lots of rest.
I tried not to get excited but eventually the day had arrived, my last in the hospital, I went around and thanked those I wanted to thank, those that were of worth during my stay, and when I actually came to thinking who they were, the list was rather smaller than I would have thought.

Sep 11th

FB. So my time here at the National Rehab Hospital is slowly coming to an end, I have two more days untill discharge, my walking is getting stronger and can now manage about 400 metres before sitting, not much you might think but a far cry to my condition just nine or ten weeks ago when I needed a hoist to get out of bed I'm now allowed to walk around the ward and also down to some therapies but I think another minimum 12 months to get back to some kind of normality.

Very little in the hand but a week ago it was zero, I now have a bit of movement in the shoulder and elbow so lie in bed most nights and mornings working on my arm, can I say thank you to all that have sent messages of support, if I have not answered you personally then I'm sorry, but thank you, excuse my language but I would not have improved diddly shit without the support of Claire, she has been my rock, my nurse, my councillor, my friend but more importantly my reason for living, I am more than a lucky man my life was turned upside down, quick example it took me just under an hour this evening to prepare my bed, get undressed and get in to it, prior to the stroke this would have taken 5 or 6 minutes max, yet when I tell Claire she just tells me how well I've done and how proud she is of me, like I said a diamond, will keep in touch, bye for now.

If you were to call into the rehab hospital, we all have our own stories, some of us are worse off than others but in the hospital, we don't see it, we may as individuals, come across obstacles we can't circumvent, but together we can do anything, our strength was our collectiveness. (A bit like the Borg in Star Trek)

Sept 12th

FB. So in a few hours I will turn my legs up into the bed in the knowledge that tomorrow I will be leaving the National Rehab Hospital and heading home to complete a journey that has taken nearly 4 months of my life a life that has changed so much..... So last night I knocked out a few numbers at the karaoke night then Annie the organiser asked me to do one last number, the chords rang out to Frank Sinatra's My Way, I stood up from my wheel chair threw my walking stick across the room and took a few steps across the floor, the cheers rang out, I sang with all my heart and when finished the crowd cheered, I looked at Annie, she clapped and jumped up and down whilst I tried to get her attention, finally she came towards me, would ya mind getting my stick I asked as I'm about to feckin Keel over, not the end I wanted and seconds later I had my stick in my hand took a bow and slipped away back up to the ward into bed to plan my escape back to Galway.

Ch.7
Stole a motorbike, jumped the steel fence and Out of the NRH

Just before I move on to the next chapter I just wanted to tell you I am writing this and hopefully a few more chapters, sitting under a parasol in Roquetas de Mar in southern Spain, I thought the fresh warm air would stir my creative juices....

So anyway the day came for me to leave the National Rehab Hospital a journey that started on the 27th May and finished on Friday 13th September, yes Friday the 13th... 110 days after my bleed, I wasn't fixed, I could walk 400 yards with a stick.... Actually they were wheeling me out to the car when I made them stop at the entrance, I said "You wheeled me in here but by feck, I am going to walk out of here," I got out of the chair declined Claire's offer of a walking stick and walked a very wobbly 25 yards to the car, Claire was still using my Chrysler 300C so there was plenty of space and comfort.
I cried as we left, not for some desire to remain at the NRH it was that I realised it wasn't the end of my journey, it was just the closing of a chapter and my tears where for the unknown chapter that lay ahead, little did I know then how hard the road would be.

We left Dublin heading West for Galway pulling in to Apple Gate Services, we pulled into the disabled parking space, and again it was like a little neon sign flashing before me saying 'YOUR LIFE IS NOW VERY DIFFERENT' I felt very obvious, although I have to say the disabled loos where very different to the regular one's, hang on I just can't put my finger on it…….. Oh yes now I have it They were feckin clean….YEE HAA, I've found one small advantage to been crook.

Just while I'm on disabled loo's, and I don't mean actually on, I'm not sitting on one now, I want to beef about able bodied folk that use disabled loo's….you know who you are, so STOP…

I wasn't prepared for home, after dreaming of being home I now found myself despising it, I wanted everything to be normal but it wasn't, it was very different.
   I stumbled and fell a few times, even breaking my toe on my left foot, didn't hurt much but by god it went a really bad yellow and black.

A lot of items, utensils, remote controls, phones etc. Flew around the house, never hitting Claire but some coming uncomfortably close, I knew I was going into depression, I was going to classes at Croi for exercise and weight control and at first it wasn't too bad, then they moved me on to another class slightly more energetic. I've seen this happen before when I was going to weight watchers, you get the one who loses a bit of weight and then become a 3rd Dan expert in weight loss.

When it came to mobility I was the most severe case in the class, but the physio's where fantastic particularly Mairéad, a small wee thing of a girl who only looked 15 but had finished her master's degree and was considering doing a PhD, after a few weeks I felt things were going the right way and then it happened, before I go on any further I want to explain this affliction which went back many years in my life.

As a young school boy of 15, I would travel on the number 16 bus into Birmingham city center on my way to school and when the nutter got on the bus he was automatically drawn to me and no effort of me trying to hide worked.

I remember one guy mumbling away as he climbed the stairs, I looked around there were plenty of empty seats but no, the inevitable happened he sat beside me, "Allo" and started rummaging in his bag, eventually pulling out a small tin, like a tea caddy, looks over at me "It's me Cat, he likes to get out", he went on to explain his cat had died some years earlier and he had it cremated, out of the corner of my eye I could see other passengers giggling as they got away with it.

But back to my class at Croi, the average age of the class was pension age and above so I was one of the younger members of the group, there was one woman, probably a good 5 stone over weight as am I, so I'm not been critical of that, but she started to have a bit of success and had lost a few pounds and all of a sudden was a complete expert advising people as they exercised where they were going wrong, you know that Harry Enfield character "Oh you don't want to do it like that".

I managed not to make eye contact for a number of weeks but in hindsight it was inevitable that it would happen, as I said I had this unexplainable draw to nutters.

She made a few comments to me but I managed to turn away and keep enough distance between us but then one week it happened, she had me in a corner "Blah blah blah came out of her mouth, she looked straight at me and I couldn't help it, I just said "sorry I'm English, I don't speak bull shit", the last two words where hidden under a cough, then as fast as I could I moved past her, the next few times I went she tried cornering me and each time I made an excuse and left, eventually I stopped going, if I'm been totally honest it wasn't just her, I felt my progress had stopped and for the first time I said to myself, "this is it pal, it's not going to change".

We had made adjustments to the house and although not plain sailing, life with a stroke was starting to become normal.
I started to make arrangements for our wedding.

Those of you who know us know we were both married previously and to my shame I have to admit I was married twice before.
 The Catholic Church and I personally think more so, the Irish Catholic Church take a very dim view on divorcees and so we could not get married in a church and had to make arrangements for a Registry Wedding.
I called the Irish Registry Office and made enquiries, on asking if we had previous marriage history, I went into detail and explained our predicament.
She then told me we would have to come up to Dublin at least 3 times, maybe as many as 5 times, we needed up to date passports, long version Birth certificates, short version no good, dates and times of court hearings and names of presiding magistrates', oh also Court room numbers plus a load of other documentation, I was so disheartened I wanted to get married as soon as possible, not just cos I loved the bones of Claire but just In case something happened to me, if you're not married in Ireland Claire has no automatic right to what's mine, it's all very complicated and archaic.

I phoned Claire, I was very dejected, I mean my first divorce was 26 years ago, how was I going to find all this information, I was putting this across to Claire whilst still looking on the Internet, "wait", I said "there is a number here for the Belfast Registry office I'll give them a call, so I hung up with Claire and phoned Belfast, explained that I was English and Claire was Irish and all about our previous marriages….. I paused and awaited a tirade of information regarding requirements, except I got, "Ah sure no bother at all, have you your last divorce papers "yes" says I, "Birth certificates", "yes" I say again, "Well get yourselves up hear and we'll marry yee, it was music to my ears.

A date was Booked and preparations began, we didn't want to take an entourage up with us we just wanted to keep it simple, so question was who to use as witnesses, it seemed easier to use 2 close friends rather than family, it wasn't a secret and if anyone wanted to come it was up to them so Claire's brother Jim and his lady travelled with us, the ceremony was in Belfast City Hall, an absolutely fabulous building steeped in history, the ceremony was simple yet lovely and within a few minutes myself and Claire were married, we had been together over 10 years, I never thought of marrying her as my past record was fairly shite but once the Registrar said the man and wife thing it all seemed so different, I grew 6 inches taller in pride as I walked out, new bride on my arm, soon she was off chatting with the other women as I slowly strolled towards the exit trying to suck in as much of the history that surrounded me.
The paintings, the photographs, I could have spent hours in there, then I spotted a fancy rope rail that formed a cordon in a section of a corridor, I walked over only to find it was the book of remembrance for the Reverent Ian Paisley, now I'm not going to make any comment on himself, I think only people who lived through the problems in Northern Ireland have a right to speak on it, but saying that, I did go over and signed the book as I felt it was a

piece of history.

We left Belfast city hall, I remember it was raining, we ended up in The Crown pub, one of, if not the oldest pubs in Belfast, across the road was the Europa Hotel once famed for been in the Guinness book of records as the most bombed hotel in the world.
I don't know if it really is true or just folklore but it is said when the bombing the hotel occurred the blast zone was set in such a way as to ensure the pub did not get damaged and still today has the most beautiful stained glass windows, a trip is a must for anyone visiting Belfast.
We ended up having our wedding meal in The Europa and a great night was had by all.

The next night was a bit different, Jim had word of a good pub for music and off we headed, I don't know Belfast well but as the taxi drove I realised we were heading towards the Falls road and eventually we alighted at a small pub called Maddens Bar, it gave us the smallest tiniest taste of what life was like in the 80's.
You had to push a buzzer to get in, someone looked you over then the door opened, the bar was fairly full and I was just about to suggest we leave when a table rose up and offered us their seats, I did feel we were been stared at, I needed the bathroom and asked Claire to give me a hand to get up, just inside the opening of the corridor to the loo's, a man was playing a fruit machine, as we reached him he stopped turned around and in a deep strong Belfast accent said "So where are you folks from", I kept my English gob closed and Claire told him "Galway," "Ah sure you's are very welcome so you are" he replied turned and continued playing the machine, after finishing my ablutions we sat back at our table, just up from us was a table with three men seated, it was obvious these

men had some standing in the bar, one of the men rose his glass and clearly mouthed 'Welcome,' all of a sudden the hum drum noise that was there when we first entered the bar suddenly returned and we were no longer the Centre of attention.

Behind me as I sat was a notice board offering Irish language lessons and Irish dancing and to the right of those was a large picture of Bobby Sands, one of the hunger strikers who died in 1981, aged just 27.

I can't imagine life there in the troubles it must have been scary, it's so sad that religion divided, communities, families and friends.

Yet as I write this book very little has changed in the world and so many have lost their life's in the name of so called religion.

Well sorry I did go off on a bit of a tangent there, we very much enjoyed our time in Belfast, on returning home to Galway, we had arranged a night in Canavan's bar in Belclare.

The bar is owned by Frank Canavan a well-known Gaelic football player who represented Galway at senior level for many years, a wonderful man and a great character in the area.

Frank runs the bar with his partner Ita

Ita would be giving instructions to Frank on what to order, who was coming what was needed etc., Frank would be walking in the opposite direction having his own conversation under his breath yet would somehow take in all that was been said, he really is a pillar of the community and he arranged food etc. for our celebrations with music from my good friend Gerry Henderson, it went on until the wee hours of the night, little did I know it would be my dad's last outing, he passed away 29th December aged 90.

CH8
Everyone's father is special, I just thought mine was extra special

I was in the sitting room with Dad one day, he started crying, I asked "what's wrong", he looked at me and said "I prayed and I prayed to God to give me your stroke and make you better again, but he didn't hear me, I would swap with you right now if I could". I had to walk out of the room because I knew I couldn't hold the tears back, I know everyone's Dad is special, but mine was extra special.

My father loved nothing more than to talk about Donegal, he would perk up and sit straight once the counties name was mentioned, he would tell me tales of his childhood and my Grandfathers life and I never grew tired of listening.

My father was the second oldest of six brothers and three sisters, one sister Bridget died at 6 months from whooping cough.

My Grandfather was James McGinley, there were 2 other James McGinley's in close proximity to each other, so my grandfather would sign his name James H McGinley, he didn't have a second name, the H coming from his father who was Hugh McGinley, this distinguished him from all the other James McGinley's but there were many James McGinley's in the surrounding towns, so amongst the larger population he was referred to as Jimmy Vicky, Vicky been his mother's maiden name, this style of naming people was very prevalent in the country side.

My Grandfather was a farmer and a fisherman, he grew enough potatoes to feed his family, any surplus would be given to neighbors in need of them, he also grew oats, these were sent to the mill to be ground into oatmeal, this would make porridge and oatmeal cakes, the straw from the oats was used to maintain the thatch on the cottage. There was very little waste in these days, when I think about how much I pay to have my recycling bin emptied, we think we are making progress, when instead we are floundering.

As for the fishing going out to sea in the 1930's, IT really was taking your life into your own hands, many of these small boats never returned, now I'm not talking about the type of boats you see on the Discovery channel, it would be a small rowing boat, with 5 or 6 men they would row out to sea cast their net, row for a couple of hours pulling the net then eventually pulling it on board by hand.

The fish would be taken home, salted and placed in a barrel, after about ten days they would be taken out of the barrel, left in the sun to dry off and cure, they would then last for many months.

My father always loved any chance to eat fish, I never really understood why till later in life when I spent more time in Donegal.

My great grandfather travelled to America where he lived and worked for several years before returning home, he would tell stories to my father and my uncles about the big cities and the tall buildings with Tram cars running along the streets, my father told me they had no idea what he was on about, the only buildings they knew were small thatched buildings and as for tramcars they had only ever seen horse and carts.

On cold winter nights they would sit around a big peat fire listening to my great grandmother singing them songs in Irish, it was my father's first language although he lost it as he grew up, when dad made the move to the UK, he deliberately changed the way he spoke, as the Donegal accent was not an easy accent on the English ear.

My Great Aunt Peggy, she was a lovely lady and would tell me tails of how she would go to my father's house as my Grandfather was a renown fiddle player, she would tell me stories of the music in the house and how she would sing and dance, when I look at it today I wonder how it was possible to raise so many people in what to me looks a small cottage but apparently it was considered a big house, so many music sessions where held there.

Sparks would fly off the hob nailed boots as they danced on the flag floors.

As I said earlier my grandfather was a great fiddle player and a very famous fiddle player called John Doherty would call to the house whenever he found himself in the area and would stay a few days with my grandad, playing the fiddle and entertaining the neighbor's in exchange for a straw mattress to sleep on and a warm meal in his belly.

Many people wanted to record John including the national television company RTE, who without his permission hid microphones at a performance he did and it disgusted him that he had been tricked and recorded by them.

John was a fiddler on the road a man who moved from town to town and house to house preserving the past and using his skill as a tinsmith, a story teller and as a musician to pay his way.

He was 4 times all Ireland fiddle player.

In an era where there were no dance halls and radio had not yet taken hold John entertained the people of the towns and villages he crossed through.
The likes of John where not called tinsmiths but whitesmiths, a man who was well dressed and well cared for, the stories told had patterns, rhythms, chorus's, they were serials that moved from night to night as the teller moved around.
In the 1930's the times were changing (hmm there's a song in that somewhere) the threads of my grandfather's culture were wearing thinner and thinner as the radio brought jazz and ragtime to a younger audience, as a new era started to poke its head up and above a society that had little change in 300 years, the days of the tinsmith, the whitesmith, the story teller where numbered, the dance halls and the showbands seen the demise of the travelling fiddler and such tales as 'The little red headed man,   the fiddler who only had one tune,   the man who lost the art of music because he didn't heed the gypsy's warning,'   gone forever with just echo's to be found here and there.

You could never be guaranteed a bed at night time and sometimes my father would make a nest of straw and sleep on the floor, I remember Steven, my nephew and Dads only grandchild asking "Grandad, which bedroom was yours",
dad roared with laughter saying "Never mind bedroom, you were lucky if you got a piece of a bed"

   one night when Dad was small a cousin of his was in the house, as ad laid out the straw the cousin filled 2 empty flour sacks for pillows, as they lay on the floor the cousin being cold got a bit too close to the fire and Dad was woken up to see his cousins pillow on fire, fortunately they were not hurt, the cousin lost some hair and an eyebrow but he was fine.

The flour sacks they used for pillows also when require were made into shirts for my dad and uncles, we think that we are the fashionable generation with our printed T-shirts, the sacks had the different names of the flour suppliers on them and if copied today would probably be seen as trendy as any designer T-shirt.

My father was a young boy of just 9 years of age when a summer storm hit Glen, it was a night in the middle of June 1933, the rains came down hard for many hours, you have to remember the cottages where built in a low area so as to gain some protection from the wind's and earlier that evening my father helped his father lay heavy chains over the thatch roof so as to hold it down but the rain did not abate, and it started to seep in the back door of the cottage, when my grandfather went out to check he was alarmed at the buildup of water on the back wall, he thought the house could be lost, inside the house were 3 of my father's aunts, they knelt down and started saying the rosary, my grandfather fetched some bales of wool, packed empty flour bags full of straw, got my father and others in the house to kneel on the bags. He then opened the back door and using the bags of wool and straw the water was directed out the front door relieving the pressure on the rear of the house, within an hour the rain stopped the sky cleared and in an instance it all seemed a distant memory, the next morning on his way to school Dad came upon one of the bridges which had been swept away in the storm, I never thought to ask him if he made it to school that day.

Of course there was a shop in the village where you could buy your provisions but most of the food Dad ate either grew on the land or was raised on the land, Dad had an uncle who was a butcher, now and again he would bring a joint of boiling meat to my grandmother, for those who may not have come across this, boiling meat was a cut from an animal, could be cow, pig or sheep, it was a tough cut that needed slow cooking to make it nice and tender, home grown vegetables, onions, potatoes and carrots and a couple of handfuls of barley would be put in the pot but here is the strange ingredient, dried fish would also be added, you see, now you go to a fancy five star restaurant and they call it Surf and Turf and food critics laud these chefs for their genius, yet my grandmother and probably her grandmother before her was cooking this in the 1800's

Dad did the usual things that a child could do in 1930's Ireland and he did have a tale or two of the shenanigans they got up to, there was a neighboring house about two miles from the home house, it was about a quarter of a mile in from the road and you had to cross a small stream to get to it the owner was a man called John McNelis or John Jack as he was known, the youngsters would congregate there as it was a remote spot out of view from their homes so they were safe from been hauled in for chores. John Jack was older than them and the lads came up with a plan that they would steal a single hen from each of the neighboring houses bring them back to John Jacks house and have a big feast.
The next night the 6 of them went out hen rustling and although John Jack said he had no hens the lads knew better and the first hen taken was his, they then sent John James McGuire, better known as JJ, a young lad who later in life would marry my father's sister, they sent him for the next hen but he came back with the

rooster, the lads knew that the lady of the house would notice the rooster missing in the morning so the rooster got a reprieve and JJ was dispatched back into the hen house eventually resurfacing with a hen, they continued their crime spree until the 6 of them had gathered up 6 hens.

They took the hens back to John Jack's house were he said he would ready them for the pot and to call back the next evening for their Hen feast, note I didn't say hen party as it could have been misconstrued as some other event, the next morning John Jack took the hens into the back bedroom just in case a neighbor would walk in on top of him whilst in the middle of plucking and cleaning them for the pot, as it happened it was raining heavy that day and because he had nothing better to be doing a neighbor called over, John Jack came down from the bedroom but left the door slightly ajar and the neighbor's dog slipped into the bedroom coming out some 5 minutes later and a trail of feathers following him but as quick as a flash John Jack said he had been beating a pillow to clean it and it burst scattering the feathers all over the room.

   Hens of that time would be nothing like the chickens you would get in today's supermarket, they would be at least twice the size so an ordinary pot would not suffice, John Jack used a large pot that was used for dyeing wool, he added potatoes, carrots, onions and barley and slowly the feast bubbled until ready, my father said the soup was so thick you could eat it with a fork, they were tucking into their illegal set menu when Willie Cunningham an older cousin who was staying with John Jack returned to the house, he was disgusted by what he found and told them so but John Jack filled another plate and placed it on the table, the aroma proved too much of a temptation and soon Willie was as guilty as the others.

So did these raiders of the night get away with it, well not quite you see the big pot they used remember me telling you it was for dyeing wool, well it hadn't been cleaned properly and they were all violently ill during the night….. don't they say God works in mysterious ways

Dad grew up without electricity and all the mod cons that go with it, so things that might seem strange to us today was just the normal way of life back then, in some parts of Ireland, the sheep would be corralled in fields surrounded by dry stone walls but in Glen the hillsides and mountain sides allowed the sheep to wander more freely, sheep are not creatures of solitude and will tend to stay together in a flock, dad enjoyed walking the hills and mountains checking or gathering the sheep, no suburban smells or noise to distract him just the noises of nature, the rustling trees or the babbling of a stream, he would heard the cows into a sheltered area it was so important to mind your animals.

It wasn't unusual for a ewe to reject a lamb or maybe the lamb was on the small side and struggled to get position on its mothers milk, so dad would look after these lambs feeding and caring for them, they would always be referred to as pet lambs, one of them grew to be quite a fine sheep but never forgot my father and some nights it would return back to the house and knock the door much like the way you or me would, dad would open the door the sheep would come in, dad would feed him a slice of bread out of his hand, contented the sheep would head out back to his woolly buddies with them none the wiser.

You wonder sometimes when I listened to dad did they have a harder or was it a more interesting life but then you hear tales like the time he caught measles, it hit the house and they all had them. And what was the cure?.... they had to drink nettle soup morning and evening, thank god for the chemist.

In Ireland the Second World war was known as 'The Emergency', Ireland remained neutral but in reality helped the British when they could, a number of ships where torpedoed by German U boats and it wasn't unusual for bodies to wash up on the Irish coast, my father remembers a number of bodies been found and taken away to be buried in the local graveyard, papers and dog tags where sent on to the British ministry of defense, 2 lifeboats from a sunken merchant ship managed to make their way to the safety of the Glen shoreline which considering the rugged coastline they were lucky to make it to shore and back to England.

Apart from some memories such as these the war did not have a real major effect in Glencolmcille

There was a shortage of coal in the UK, as although it was a protected occupation, many miners joined up to fight for their country, Ireland used to import coal from the UK but this supply suffered during the war, but it meant an opportunity for my father and he set off to Kildare in 1943 to work in the Turf camps, they lived in temporary huts walking 2 miles a day to work, working a 12-hour day 6 days a week for 35 shillings a week, this was actually good money for the time, some of the men gambled playing pitch and toss but my father was a cagy man and would sometimes pick up bargains such as a smart leather jacket from those that had lost their money gambling.

Dad left his home in Donegal and travelled to Britain in the 1950's on what he referred to as a government ticket, the Second World War had not long finished and Britain were looking for labor to rebuild the country's infrastructure.

He was given a ticket for the boat and five pounds plus documentation regarding the promise of a job in the Yorkshire mines, Donegal men had a great reputation as miners but dad had heard enough tales in Glen about the hardships of being a miner and on arriving to the UK, he made a Bee line for Birmingham, there wasn't a man crossing the Irish Sea that did not have the address of someone they either knew or were related to that would give them a bed until they got themselves sorted.

Dad had many tales of the characters he came across during his time in Birmingham, I have a couple of small tales as a taster.

One day my father was working in the Bull Ring, a new massive shopping Centre built in the 1960's, he was working away when an old friend from his time on the buses was passing by and stopped to chat to Dad for the books sake well call him Mick, after chatting to Dad for half an hour Mick looked down the road to see an extremely large queue had now formed at his intended bus stop, now due to the major works that where ongoing around the area the bus stop was one of those temporary ones with a steel round base to hold it up, Mick said his good bye's to my father, walked down to the bus stop, picked it up walked up the road about 10 feet, put it down then stood beside it, then the whole queue without saying a word just moved in unison and formed an orderly line behind Mick.

As I briefly mentioned earlier, Dad worked on the trams in Brum, now I'm not an electrician but I'll try and explain the way it worked, a large pole on top of the tram touched a high powered electricity cable, it all formed a single circuit, the cable the pole the tram and the tracks so, if a trams pole came away from the overhead wire the circuit was broken and not only that tram but all the trams on that track stopped.

As a driver if your pole disconnected from the power source, it was considered a serious failure and you were required to write up a report as to why it happened, one of the reasons it could happen was if a driver was taking a bend too fast, something one of my father's friends Micky Finnegan had a habit of doing.

Micky had a reputation for writing very long reports as to why the pole came off, this could range from a fictitious child running across the tracks to inclement weather shaking the tram etc.

One day whilst my father was in the canteen with Micky one of the inspectors came in carrying a bundle of papers in his hand, he came up to Micky waving the papers under his nose saying "Christ sake Micky can you make these reports a bit simpler "Not a problem boss" says Micky "I'll make sure I'll do that".

Dad told me it was just a few days later the pole came off Micky's tram but he was good to his word and kept his report short

"POLE OFF, POLE ON AGAIN"
                    Finnegan

On 22nd December, 14 days after dad hit 90, he took ill
He got up as normal, had his porridge, walked into the living room, sat in his chair and had what we think was a Mini stroke, a TIA, maybe God heard him when Dad prayed to take my stroke but he didn't get the full message.

Mom called myself and Claire over from the main part of the house, we found dad slumped in his favorite chair, an electrical recliner, he really loved that chair.

He was conscious, but not able to open his eyes, he managed to tell Claire that he couldn't move his arms or legs.

Dad had spoken to Claire over the years about not wanting to die in a hospital, that's why we built the extension onto the house, so we could mind the pair of them.

Dad had been diagnosed with CLL, a form of Leukemia and had

been attending the Galway Hospice 1 day a week for over 2 years, he loved going and the staff and nurses doted over him, he came home one day with his first ever professional haircut, up till then my mother had always cut his hair, he would be looking in the mirror laughing as he preened himself another time he came home with a flower arrangement in one of those foam oasis giving it to mom who said "I had to wait 63 years for him to give me flowers" and dad just laughed but the one thing that totally amazed us is at the age of 88 we found out he had a natural talent for painting, and he completed three of which not only are we very proud as a family but also very protective of.

I was with dad sitting beside him, I'm not ashamed to admit it I was crying my eyes out, Dad managed to just about open his eyes, he looked at me and in a whisper he said "It's all right Jon, don't be crying, I've had a great life and if it's my time then that's ok" that just made me worse but before I could get any more upset, Claire returned, she said to Dad, "it's alright Francie an ambulance is on the way", again his eyes opened, "am I going into hospital" he asked" "No" said Claire " you're going to the hospice" "oh, that's ok" he said and closed his eyes.

He woke the next morning and was quite bright and chatty, he had a small bit of movement in the arms but not the legs, at first I was quite upbeat thinking we might yet take him home, but it wasn't to be and one week after he was admitted he died, thankfully we got to spend one last Christmas with him and he even managed a small bit of Christmas dinner.

I gave great thought to what I wanted to say at his funeral, I felt I had a very short time to get across what a wonderful man he was. I stood up at the alter addressing the congregation, I told them how

they knew my father as a very hard working man who left the small village of Glencolmcille in the county of Donegal worked as a Tram driver in Birmingham and bus driver after the trams where phased out then spending many years working in construction, but what they didn't know was my dad was a master of many trades.
*He was a taxi driver, who drove myself and my brother anywhere we needed to go…. No Charge
*He was a banker who when approached for a loan always had funds readily available with zero repayment option…... No charge
*A master mechanic who thought nothing of pulling on his overalls and getting my car going again…… No charge.

Since my stroke my emotional state has changed, I could be watching a 1940's black and white movie where the wife of the hero gets a telegraph to say her husband is missing presumed dead then 5 minutes later he walks into the room into her arms and I uncontrollably burst into tears, it can be very embarrassing if it happens when I'm in company, I tell you this because after Dad died, the days prior to his funeral and the day of his funeral, I never shed a tear, I became confused I kept asking what was wrong with me, subconsciously did I not care that my dad, the man I looked up to all my life was lying dead in his coffin, would I start blabbing at the altar when I was reading my epitaph to my father but no, not one single tear left me, the wake the funeral, the gathering in Canavan's afterwards, nothing, then about three days later I was talking to Claire and just burst into an unstoppable tirade of tears, it just hit me like a boxers right hand my father, my Dad was dead, gone forever.
I know this sounds stupid but I just thought my father would never die.

107

CH9
Life? CAN IT EVER BE NORMAL AGAIN?

"Can we go on holiday"?   a question raised by Claire, I looked into flying after a stroke on the Internet, it gave some mixed messages but whilst on a general check up with my doctor, I asked his opinion and he gave me the green light, we travelled to Spain to an area I had not been to before, Almeria, to anyone reading this book who might have any sort of problems with walking can I just say Almeria is perfect as it's very flat and much more accessible to invalids or elderly people, actually I think I now qualify for both of those categories but it very nearly never happened.

We arrived at the airport found the desk for mobility impaired persons, they went through our paperwork and off we went with boarding cards and through to the departure gate, I was totally fixated on trying to go to the loo for a jimmy riddle, Claire was busily sipping water asking me if I wanted any, I was so thirsty yet was even more paranoid of needing the loo during the flight as I knew there would be no chance of me getting to it, it was whilst we were sitting at the departure gate I was looking at the boarding cards and Claire's seat number was 27C whilst mine was 27F,   I was concerned at first as I knew I needed Claire with me for assistance but then we agreed it would get sorted once we got on the plane.

At last a call went out for boarding, Claire went up to one of the stewards to enquire on how we board, the girl showed us to some chairs close to the departure gate telling us to sit there and she would call us when required, eventually as most of the passengers where boarding we got the nod from the girl to board.

Off I went following this guy down a ramp eventually exiting the airport to a waiting airport vehicle where we got on to find some other passengers already in it, it was like a small cabin on the back of a truck that when we got out to the plane, the cabin rose vertically on a scissors style lift up to the aircraft doorway, yee HAA I'm on the plane, a big smile crossing my face, we showed our boarding cards to the steward pointing out how the seats where not together, he just told us not to worry and just sit together.

So we sat, me in 27F the window seat, they like to put the mobility impaired people on the inside so as in an emergency we don't hinder the evacuation of others, nice, Claire sat in 27E next to me, we were just settled in when a woman (if I can call her that) arrived at our row, she looked at her ticket looked at the seating numbers then at Claire saying in a loud Dublin 4 voice "You are sitting in my seat", Claire explained my condition saying we needed to sit together but before she could finish her words the woman said "I'm not interested in anything you have to say, just get out of my seat", Claire was becoming upset as others where now rubber necking to see what all the commotion was about, I nodded to Claire it's ok, I'll be alright and Claire got up from her chair visibly upset, as this was going on the husband of the woman was trying to persuade his wife to move seats but she was insistent that was her seat and she was having it.

At first I thought maybe I would be ok but I soon realized any small movement I needed to make I needed Claire's help.
I tried to make a plea to the woman only to be told "you have no

reason to speak to me so DON'T" all this time the cabin crew were getting the aircraft ready for departure, I pushed the call button in the overhead panel, a member of the crew came down, "sorry" I said "but I need to get off the plane, I'm not able to travel on my own I need my wife's assistance throughout the flight" again the husband was trying to persuade his wife to move but again she refused, eventually the crew member just said "Excuse me madam but it appears you have been issued the wrong seat, you should be in seat 27C, eventually the woman mumbling and looking at me giving me daggers got up from the seat and moved, the flight took off

We arrived in Almeria and I remember the feeling of warmth enter the aircraft as the doors opened and that unmistakable smell you get associated with a hot climate, I felt good, my stroke, the furthest thing from my mind but that soon changed as it came our turn to disembark from the aircraft, three and a half hours sitting in the smallest space Ryan Air can get away with, speaking of which I read a report a few years back that Ryan air was looking at a layout for short hall craft where you don't actually have a seat but perch your backside on a small perching seat whist holding a strap as you sometimes might on an underground tube train.
Also just another point of interest, in Dublin Ireland they cut down the width of some of the roads into the center so as to form Bus lanes, the only transport allowed in these lanes where bus's bicycles and Taxi's so what does Michael O Leary do, owner and chief exec of Ryan Air, he pays 50,000 euros for a taxi license so he can drive in these lanes, I suppose if I had his money maybe I would do the same.

Back to my journey, after 3 hours seated in a very constricted environment Claire was trying to help me up, pulling, dragging, a bit of cursing too and the disappearance of my underpants during this struggle and I was out, like a sardine leaving his tin for the last time, out the aircraft door, through the official controls and then been squeezed into a taxi, it all felt so good such a far cry from been hoisted out of my hospital bed in slings to go to the loo.

I love the journey from the airport to the hotel, it's that journey of wonderment, looking the same as home, the roads the signs, the tree's etc. yet everything looking completely different, you knew you were away.

Soon we arrived at the hotel and things started to go wrong despite writing a letter and sending 2 emails (none of which were replied to) regarding my disability, Claire was handed door cards for a room on the fourth floor, I know it's awful ignorant to expect everyone else in the world to speak English but most Spanish hotels we had used over the years had somebody that could speak English, after an arduous flight Claire was in no mood to argue but stood her ground repeating "we have contacted you 3 times to request we get a disabled apartment on the ground floor, now just sort it out and give me the apartment" by this time my stroke leg was getting very sore from standing.

  I felt so bad that I was abandoning her but I had to sit or I would be adding to her problems, this particular hotel we later found out was only that year pushing itself to the English and Irish markets but eventually a young very polite Swedish receptionist came to Claire's aid enquiring with regards to the problem and quickly found our emails and then reallocated us an apartment, ground floor, disabled bathroom…. The Eagle or in my case the Doe Doe had landed.

Life seemed pretty good, we were enjoying the sunshine, the wine, the food, and the wine,(no it's not a typo) it took a bit of forward planning but I got into the pool, monitored by a very overzealous Claire who gave one of those deadly death ray stares to any child who came within 5 feet of me.

Meeting people on holiday is usually a lovely experience as everyone is in good form, I was sitting under the parasol one day when an old boy in his 60's walked by with an entourage of about 10 women following behind, (an all-girl football team) I looked around, you could nearly hear the cog's turning in the brains of some of the other men folk as they looked down at their wives then back at the lovely ladies following this pensioner and minding him all day, a complete look of wonderment on their faces.

I had met a couple of the girls earlier, Beth, whose father was leading the entourage, Kay and Sarah 2 girls who played for the football team in England, on a beano with their buddies for a bit of fun and relaxation, it was just great craic watching the tongues hanging out from some of the other male holiday makers as Steven got completely spoilt.

It's strange when you're on holiday, you pass someone in the restaurant not having a clue who they are only to meet them 10 minutes later in the bar and start chatting like long lost friends, it was in that situation that we met Pam and Stewart, on entering the bar we surveyed the room looking for a table, then spotted Stewart who moved a chair so as to motion us to join them.

I mention them because a couple of days later we, without meaning to, we got Stewart into a spot of trouble with his wife.
We were having a drink chatting away about the hotel and the

resort when Stewart mentioned how they had been on a walk along the beach pathway (too small to class it as a promenade) We said we had gone that direction ourselves, "How far did you manage to go" asked Stewart, Claire said," we stopped just before we got to the nudist beach".

Well Pam's face was a picture "A nudist beach?" "Yes" said Claire, it's just after the nice benches where all the trees and the cover from the sun was"

Pam turning to Stewart, "So that's why you wanted to go up there" "Hang on " says Stewart, "it was your bloody idea to go up that way" "Yes it was, yes it was" says Pam "but you never tried to stop me", it was turning into an episode of Gavin and Stacy, poor old Stewart was in a no win situation, but it didn't stop us mentioning it now and again during the holiday.

Another interesting trait was been able to tell where the new arrivals had come from when we would go into breakfast.

For example, if all of a sudden there was a big queue for the fresh crusty bread It usually meant a plane load from France had arrived, a queue for the cold meats meant the Russian plane came in, we always knew when the Ryan air flight had arrived as there would be a long queue for the bacon and eggs.

There was a bar called The Manhattan just across the road, so whilst having some Tapas at the Oasis bar we decided the Manhattan was going to be our choice of venue for the night, an elderly lady called Connie who we had run into in the hotel passed our table, she stopped "Hello" she said in a lovely soft welsh accent "would you mind if I joined you", we had finished our meal so we pulled out a chair and Connie sat down "I've had enough of those two miserable buggers" she said "but Connie, I thought they were your sisters" I returned, "they are " she said "but I don't get on with them, never have" "so why do you go on holiday together" Claire enquired "well you have to, don't you, I mean where family, but it doesn't mean you have to like each other", now I'll just point out Connie was an 84 year old grey haired granny like creature "Have you never got on" I enquired,

"No, not really, can't stand the bastards if truth be known" anyway I ordered Connie a drink, on finishing it, I announced that we would be heading off now to the Manhattan club, thinking Connie would be saying good night, but instead her face lit up, she looked at Claire and said "Oh can I come with you please, I could do with a good night out".

So off we went with Connie in tow into the club, now it wasn't a trendy night club, and this particular night was a Karaoke night ran by a number of locals and I have to say they put in the effort and the night was going well, I could see Connie chatting away to Claire incessantly and I eventually got pulled in to listen.

A chap got up to do his piece on stage, something from the sixties, I'd say this lad was well into his late 70's, Connie took a look spun around and said "He's a bit of all right" then with a pained expression on her face said "do you think he'll want sex, because I have a Vagifem Up inside me", I couldn't believe what I was hearing, this person that I thought was a quiet little old lady was raving to go, anyone over 70 was getting attention from her, I was red faced listening to her, but thinking about it, she was spot on, dead right, just because you look like a pensioner you don't have to act like one.

The next afternoon we were sitting around the pool when Connie and her sisters walked by, Claire said "did you have fun shopping" Connie stopped the sisters kept moving and again in her soft Welsh lilt turned to Claire " I've a shocking headache this morning and to tell you the truth those two did nothing to help it, moan moan moan

they have, like a badly tuned saxophone".
We didn't see Connie again she and her sisters headed off the next morning, I hope she's keeping well bless her

After the holiday was over I found myself back in the familiar surroundings of home.
Home is a small town called Tuam, for those of you who don't know it, it is pronounced Choom, a small town that has the claim of being the smallest city in the world, because, in the UK, the distinction between a large town and a small city was due to a British town usually of major size or importance having the status of an episcopal, a bishop and where there is a Bishop, there is usually a Cathedral and Tuam has 2, one protestant and one Catholic.

CH 10

Tuam is also the home town of 'The Saw Doctors'.

The Saw Doctors are an Irish rock band. Formed in 1986 in Tuam, County Galway. They have achieved eighteen Top 30 singles in The Republic of Ireland including three number ones. Their first number one, "I Useta Lover," topped the Irish charts for nine consecutive weeks in 1990, and still holds the record for the country's all-time biggest-selling single, stick that in yer pipe and smoke it Bono.

Renowned for their live performances, the band has a cult following, especially in Ireland, the United Kingdom, and the United States. On 15 February 2008, they received a Lifetime Achievement Award at the Meteor Ireland Music Awards.

I'm sure you've heard the well-known quotation from Andy Warhol, "Everyone will have 15 minutes of fame, It does derive from Warhol but his actual line he used was somewhat different - "In the future everybody will be world famous for fifteen minutes.".
Now I'm not world famous although I still have time and maybe in a quiet moment I might go on a culling spree of politicians but I did get my 15 minutes of fame in Galway, not quite worldwide, a young

man by the name of Paul Cunniffe, a cousin of my cousin if you can follow that, a very talented Singer song writer, was tragically killed in an accident on a building site in Galway, he was very much a part of the Tuam music scene.
The Saw Doctors decided to play a fund raising gig in order to help out Paul's family, at this time in my life I was still working for Galway County Council but I also had a music shop called

'Music N Mayhem' Leo Moran from The Saw Doctors came into the shop with tickets for the gig, asking if we would sell them and then it happened, Leo just said "Do ya fancy doing a few of Paul's song's", We had been selling a CD of Paul's music in the shop to raise funds for Paul's family, I was blown away, of course I said "yes".

The weekend came I nervously went to Campbell's Tavern in Cloughanover, Galway, for a quick rehearsal for the show later that night, I had been playing guitar for many years, had stood on stage in front audiences in England and Ireland yet standing on the stage with these guys, lads I'd admired and travelled to many parts of the country to see, I was as nervous as a cow at a barbecue convention.
The lads where very kind to me yet I still felt very much intimidated standing on there with my musical hero's.
Anthony 'Anto' Thistlethwaite a multi-instrumentalist was on bass and not as familiar with Paul's CD as the others, so he positioned himself right in front of me so as to follow the songs chords by watching my fingering, I was bricking it I mean here was a former member of The Waterboys, another of my all-time favorite bands his six foot plus frame towering over me and a complete look of 'What the Feck' on his face, you see my hands are on the small side, pity my belly didn't follow suit, so I use unusual fingering on

some chords causing confusion to the big man.

Relief kicked in as rehearsal came to an end, I was to play three songs on the night and I stood nervously in the crowd that evening as Padraig Stevens and Seamie Rutledge set the night in motion, then at last I was called up on stage the minute I got up there my nerves just slipped away, I just loved the stage, the songs went well, I took my bows and exited stage left, the night was completed with me joining all the musicians from the night for a four song encore, the crowd went wild and my short fifteen minutes of fame came to a conclusion, no drugs, no drink, no groupies, no party just great memories, made even better when the sound engineer from the night, he gave me a recording of the concert.

A few years later, I recorded my own album 'Time to go lakes' and I used one of the songs from the night as the last track on the album.

Music became a big part of my life as I played many of the bars in Tuam, Reapy's Select bar was one of the first regular places I played, myself and friends Gerry Henderson (guitar & Vocals), Alan Flynn (percussion) and Turps on Mandolin, there was no fixed line up and other musicians would sit in and join us, as the night progressed the pint's kicked in, not just with ourselves but also the crowd and for what was a small pub we would have the people singing, dancing and rocking, the landlord loved us.

We got requests from other pubs and bars in Tuam and Galway city, we became a tight outfit, we learned from one another we really improved and even if I say so myself we were bloody good. Then we suddenly found ourselves playing 5 nights a week, for a while it was ok but then after doing it week after week, month after month it seemed it wasn't fun anymore, Gerry would say "When we are being paid there is always someone to tell you when you must start, when you can finish and what you can play" he was so right, sometimes we would be out on a night out, you know the one's that just become better as the night goes on, we would pop home for the guitars or pick them up from whatever bar we played the previous night and have an impromptu music session, it never mattered where we were, there wasn't a landlord in Galway that would stop a session, they may even throw down a few rounds of drink to keep us going and we decided what we played.

Gerry went to the doctor one time complaining of a sore throat, he had it for a number of weeks and was concerned, the doctor on checking his throat made an appointment for a more thorough check and the worst was confirmed Gerry had cancer of the tongue, something I had never heard of, he was admitted to Hospital in Dublin and underwent the most amazing bit of surgery I ever heard of.
They had to cut out his tongue and I mean right down the back of his throat, then they took a piece of muscle from his wrist as it was closest in texture of the tongue and rebuilt his tongue but then they had to take muscle from the thigh to put into the wrist so his hand would work as normal, it never ceases to amaze me what these medical practitioners can do.
At first when I went in to visit Gerry, he communicated via a pad and pencil but as the days passed and with the help of a speech and language therapist he started talking again, at first his speech was difficult to understand but as time went by he got better at speaking and I got better at understanding him.
Eventually the day came for him to leave, I travelled from Galway up to Dublin to pick him up and I was helping him with his belongings when one of the nurses called in all bright and sparkly

she handed Ger a piece of paper saying, "Here you are Gerry there's details of your appointments, you have to see the speech and language therapist on the Wednesday and the Consultant wants to see you on the Thursday".

Gerry looked down at the appointment slip, then looked up at the nurse saying "Do you think I have a helicopter, I live in Tuam" and without saying another word just held the appointment slip out in front of himself, sheepishly the nurse took the slip, walked out the room returning just some 10 minutes later with both appointments scheduled for the same day, I knew then that Gerry may have lost his tongue but not his sharpness.

At this stage I had my music shop in Tuam so I took the opportunity as we were in Dublin to pick up some CD's stock whilst also going for a bite to eat at a real Dublin Greasy Spoon Café, it was one of those proper old fashioned cafes' in one of the industrial estates that had about 8 women just constantly cooking bacon, eggs, sausage, beans, black pudding and white pudding whilst another 2 women took the orders.

Gerry sat and a full Irish breakfast was soon in front of him, it was something I had not realized but Ger told me he had no taste sensation in his new tongue but as he tucked into his breakfast his facial expression changed and he got a bit excited as something resembling taste was filtering through and the Ger grin, something that is similar to what you would see on a cheeky 5-year-old spread across his face.

We travelled on to the company that I used to buy the shops CD's from, Ger came with me and as a man who has a serious love of music he quickly immersed himself in the vast array of musical spectrums that lay in front of him, the proverbial kid in the candy store.

Back in Tuam life was going ok, and although I had been playing gigs, Turps had some business to attend to and gave music a break and obviously Gerry was in no position to sing, the magic was gone, we were the sum of the parts, you take one away and maybe the magic can recover but take 2 away and it no longer existed, it wasn't that I was short of work it just wasn't there, the buzz, the fun, the sound, it was gone…

Then one Sunday afternoon, many months later I went into a small bar called The Rustics, a small but much loved Tuam pub.
Gerry was inside and low and behold he had a guitar in his hand and this man who had lost his tongue started playing and singing, I could not believe it, I could feel the tears welling up in my eyes and once more we enjoyed and played the Tuam scene until we drifted apart, it was getting to a point where my marriage to Karen was heading down a deep hole and my head was not in a music place.

It never ceased to amaze me the level of recovery Gerry made from his health issues and the memory of it helped inspire me not to give up hope in my own recovery to where it reached a point in time where the two of us found ourselves in Canavans bar Belclare, the reason we were there? It was to celebrate my marriage to Claire, I had asked Gerry if he would bring his guitar and knock out a few tunes.
I remember Claire asking me would I be ok watching Gerry, she knew how hard it had been for me when I sold my Guitars, selling them was the final acknowledgement that I was never going to get the use of my left arm and hand again but I sat with Claire, listening to Gerry even joining in on some of the songs, then Gerry handed

me a harp (harmonica) and I suddenly felt alive, I was a part of it again, the magic that flows between us whilst playing music, it wasn't there when I was just singing, the fact that I have a better voice than him is neither here nor there….. (oops that's going to cost me a few beers) and since that night I've sat in with him a few times enjoying his talent and enhancing it when I thought necessary (That'll be a Guinness for Henderson) I really should learn to keep my gob shut, it would be much cheaper. I still hope to get back to playing live music again I'll just have to adapt to what I can use.

CH11
FAME DIDN'T CALL ME
SO I HAD TO GET A PROPER JOB

I went back to college in my early 20's studying construction engineering and got myself a job with the now defunct Wimpey construction one of the biggest contractors in the Midlands, my first big contract I worked on was the Birmingham International Convention Centre, not to be confused with the National Exhibition Centre out by the airport the International Convention Center is in the heart of the city and it was only in 2014 some 28 years later that I went back to see the finished product, it was very strange as people working in the shops and the Centre along with all the members of the public were buzzing around getting on with their day whilst I was slowly walking along looking about thinking, "Oh, I remember that column its 18mm out of position, oh and that stairs we had to rebuild that 3 times and the wall to the left should have had a 25mm chamfer on top, it was so easy to slip back 28 years and immerse myself in the rows, the laughs, the camaraderie even the fights we had.

I think the wonderful thing about working in construction is it changes and evolves all the time, a production factory takes the same ingredients and turns it into a finished product, it does that on Monday on Tuesday, on every day, whilst we started off with a

blank canvas and developed it into something special.
The owner might own it, the Architect dreamt it, the Civil Engineer figured out how it could be built but it was the construction company that made it come true.

The International Convention Centre, Birmingham or as it was better known as the ICC, attracted media interest.

We had a number of cranes on the site but one of them was the tallest free standing crane in Europe so we had a visit from Central Television, a lovely young lady came out with a camera man climbed up the crane and did an interview with the driver, I can't remember his first name but his surname was Walsh so I shall now refer to him as Walshie.

The route up to the crane was not via a single long ladder but a vertical ladder with resting platforms every so often, the piece went out on TV which got the chatter going in the canteen, talking about the stunning views and asking who had gone up, by the end of that week I was the only staff member who had not gone up and it was becoming a bit irritating having to constantly answer the same question, "Have you been up yet?"
Eventually the day came, I had a bit of free time so up I started, up to platform one then platform two by this time I was about one third of the way up.
It amazed me how much the tower of the crane was moving, if it didn't move it would snap, I understood and was aware of that but was still taken back by the amount it did move, off I went, platform 3 then heading to platform 4 a really strong gust of wind caught me off balance, I quickly grabbed the ladder with all my might and at the same time my hard hat toppled off my head and I watched as it

hit a couple of the cranes cross members before bouncing outwards and falling down to the ground below, I just thought ok, that could be me, you're going to get stick for this McGinley and slowly I started to edge myself downwards, vertical ladders are horrid because the proper way to climb or descend them is to lean back as far as you can with your arms stretched out at full length but after my fright, my mode of descent was step by step clinging on to the ladder like a thick piece of grease eventually reaching the bottom and only getting about 0.5 of a second before I was barracked by the watching crowd followed by a further 2 weeks of abuse in the canteen but eventually the lads got bored with it and it became a distant memory.

Walshie only came down at lunch times so in effect he could be up there 5 hrs. between breaks and you quickly learned not to spend too much time close to the base of the crane as you might think you felt a few rain drops only to look up at Walshie laughing as he emptied his pee bottle over the edge.

He also loved to flick his teabags out of his window, in the summer time he might catch a shirtless lad on his back, very painful and you'd suddenly here a scream and you'd look up to see one of the carpenters spinning around, foul language filling the air and his back covered in tea leaves, he actually got me on my hard hat one day, I was amazed how much came out of one tea bag.

The crane was controlled by the operator and a man on the ground called a 'Banksman', the banksman would be in touch with the operator by radio giving him instructions and between the operator and the banksman they could literally drop a large crate or a piece of formwork to within a few millimeters of where it needed to be.
If there was no radio there were nationally agreed hand signals, the banksman would wear a different colour hard hat and safety vest to

all other employees so as to make him more recognizable and easier to spot for the crane operator.

One day a small 2-ton dumper was been loaded on the back of a flat back wagon, the crane driver lifted the dumper and landed it right on the wagon, the wagon driver threw a retaining strap over it to secure it , the banksman got up to release the chains but got distracted when someone came onto the sight asking about a delivery he had to make, the banksman jumped off the flat back and started giving the guy instructions on where to go, meantime the driver of the flat back got in his cab, started up and proceeded to head off the site with the tallest tower crane in Europe still attached to his load.

The crane driver sounded his claxon and was screaming down the radio, one of the site managers in his office had a radio on charge and switched on, he heard the commotion and dashed out the office and stopped the truck, by this time a number of people were also in pursuit of the truck, I have heard or at least thought I'd heard every bit of profanity in the English language but I heard a few new words that day coming from the crane driver.

All he could do was let out the line as quickly as he could as the truck drove across the site; this crane could lift 20t up in the air vertically no problem but truck pulling him sideways would have collapsed the crane in an instant, the minute the truck was brought to a halt Walshie started out of his cabin as I said earlier there were platforms along the ladder so you could get off the ladder and rest but Walshie came down that ladder faster than a fireman down his pole, at the same time, the banksman threw off his jacket let go of the radio and just disappeared off the site, it was 3 weeks before he showed his face again by that time Walshie had calmed down and he got his job back and although you would think that's a bit dangerous, he confronted his job with a very different attitude.

In all there was five tower cranes on the site and even though that might sound a lot they were constantly in demand and you could sometimes have to wait 2 hours for a lift but one day whilst my turn had just come I was telling the banksman what was needed then I heard the crackle on his radio and a voice said "Mandy's doing her exercises" and all of a sudden the tower cranes all turned one by one in the same direction pointing towards a tower block, so I said to the banksman "Where the fuck has my crane gone and who the fuck is Mandy", he looked at me and smiled, "Mandy, well that's what we call her, every morning she does her aerobic exercises in her living room in the nip", when I looked up each crane driver had a pair of binoculars all watching Mandy's show.

A year or so later after my failed attempt at climbing the tower crane, I decided to make an attempt on a much smaller 30m crane, also the ladders were angled in approx. 25 foot stages, it was a much easier climb, so off I went with camera in hand and feeling much braver.
The crane was being used to concrete a wall, the crane would have a 1 cubic meter skip which would be filled with concrete and weighing in at approx. 2.7 tonnes it would be lifted up to the concrete gang and opened up, depositing the concrete into the wall formwork.
I had reached the drivers cabin, now you have to remember it was not designed for 2 people but there was room for me to crouch behind the driver, I was just squeezing myself passed the driver when all of a sudden I was thrown over the driver landing in the back, I screamed like a baby, I thought something had hit the crane and my time was up, then I heard the crane driver he was

screaming but not with fright but laughing his head off, by this time I had righted myself and was looking over his shoulder him still laughing he said "It's just the skip of concrete" what he meant was the skip which was right out at the end of his jib had just been emptied meaning 2.7t of concrete suddenly taken off the jib resulting in the crane basically springing backwards, I was up there for another 5 or 6 skip loads and even though I knew it was coming it still unnerved me.

I was glad to get down onto terra firma and although I worked on a number of jobs with tall tower cranes I never went up one again.

Due to the size of the contract it did attract media attention and we received visits from a number of dignitaries.
We got word that Prince Charles would be coming and I was amazed at the amount of work that was put in to his visit.

I was working one night a bit later than usual catching up on paperwork all of a sudden my office door burst open, I spun around to see two uniformed armed officers standing in the doorway, their guns were holstered, "What the fuck are you doing here" one of them shouts, I was so taken back I just sort of uttered "blah blah blah" "We were informed the offices are closed", he shouted while his buddy looking over his shoulder also kept looking down the corridor by now I had gathered some composure, "I'm just catching up on paperwork", I said,
The man looked at me "Name", I told him and he produced some papers scanned through them stopping at my name "Right, ok, we need you to leave immediately, I came so close to just saying "can I just finish this off" when my brain clicked in and I just left down my pen picked up my coat and walked past the two officers.
His Royal Highness Prince Charles was only coming for a 2hr visit

yet every manhole in the vicinity was checked and once satisfied the lids replaced and a lead seal put on them, all the offices were checked by special branch officers and dogs.

One side of the site was bordered by a canal and it was dragged and checked by divers then on the day of his arrival you could see police marksmen stationed on top of the surrounding buildings.

The royal family take a lot of stick from some quarters but it's not a nice life, every day planned out to the last minute many years in advance.

So the day arrived and Charlie turned up on time, the site was very mucky yet a clean layer of stone encircled the site, I mean you couldn't have the man getting his shoes dirty.

As he was taken around one of the senior management was giving him the spiel and pointing here and there explaining where the concert hall would be where the theatre would be etc.

The Senior Director turned around only to find Charles was not there, he had walked down a temporary stairwell with his security team in tow to where 3 Jamaican carpenters had positioned themselves to watch proceedings. Charles started talking to them offering his hand and I remember the lads wiping their hands on their clothing trying to ensure they did not present a dirty hand to the future King of Britain, I thought fair play he wanted to talk to the guys involved in the job and not just listen to a well-practiced speech by a director who had never set foot on the job before, eventually he reached us, all the site management staff were lined up to meet him, he must find this a very boring part of his work been introduced to people he does not know and will never meet again yet he had a different question to each of us.

I was introduced as the senior site Engineer at which point he asked me 'Had I ever put a part of the building in the wrong place', I

could feel the eyes of the other staff burning into the back of my head, my reply was "All the time sir" and he had a little giggle, eventually he was introduced to Peter Lewis the senior Forman, "So Peter, how are you doing for labour", "Why" said Peter, "Are you looking for a job", the senior brass threw their eyes up to heaven, mortified and embarrassed yet the Prince just smiled and looked at Peter saying, "I wouldn't mind trying my hand at brickwork" to which Peter replied, "Leave your name at the office and if we get an opening I'll give you a call".
I think the senior brass were pleased to just get passed us.

A small bit later that day I was walking along the site offices when Prince Charles's Limo drove slowly past me and despite the darkened window I could easily make out the shape of Charles. His Royal Highness put his hand up and acknowledged me, I just stopped in my tracks and gave him a big thumbs up…. Me, yes little old me got a wave from the next king of Britain.

Another memory I have of this project was when the Department of Social Welfare raided the site with a contingent of approx. 40 police officers, as stated earlier the site was surrounded by an eight-foot fence on three sides and the canal on the fourth and much to my amazement when the Welfare people came on site at least 10 or more lads leapt the small four-foot fence and dived into the canal to get away, they must have been desperate because that canal water was filthy with muck and especially with diesel from the canal barges.
Some lads hid in the steel containers, under tarpaulins anywhere they could, in my innocence I was amazed at how many people were trying to screw the system.

The next big project I worked on was The West Orchard Shopping Centre, this was right in the heart of Coventry to the point where the fenced hoarding was nearly on the line of the exterior of the building, which meant space was at a premium.

Due to this we hired the 2nd floor on a 4 floor building and turned it into our main office, the ground floor and first floor was a lady's fashion outlet, the shop manager was also the building manager a lovely fine looking lady called Anna, at this time in my life I had just turned 30, divorced and as gullible as a puppy, every time I would have to see Anna, she'd give me a big hug and a kiss, so puppy thought Aahh she likes me, I mean she was blonde, good looking, dressed really well (then again she did run a fashion outlet).

One day, puppy, sorry I, had to go up to the top floor, it was a photographers studio, we had a lot of material, timber, plywood, plasterboard sheets etc. For the new office and I wanted to land them on the roof with the tower crane and take them down to the second floor using the stores stock elevator, this would save us causing any convenience to the shop below but it did mean a bit of pulling and dragging plus a good few labors plodding about the place and I just wanted to clear it with Anna so she fully understood what we were doing.

I went to the shop looking for Anna only for one of the other girls to tell me she was on the top floor.

Up to the top floor, rang the doorbell, a lad with three cameras around his neck, in a flash (no pun intended) I surmised he was the photographer, I explained who I was and that I wanted to see Anna, "Come on in" he says "we will be finished in a minute", in I go and there was Anna "I won't be long sweetheart, just take a seat" I stood frozen to the spot, Anna surrounded by the photographer's lamps, was lying back on a rug as starker's as the day she was born.

Anna spotted my obvious surprise and coyness, "Come on sweetheart don't be shy" as she beckoned me over, I was a normal hot blooded male yet I found myself looking up at the ceiling as I walked along and I'm sure as bright red as a cherry.

The session ended and Anna putting on a thin dressing gown came over to me, my uncomfortableness was very obvious as she used a finger to stroke me under the chin, playing on my shyness "Now what can I do for you sweetheart", I know I explained what we needed to do with the delivery but I'm not sure which octave range my voice used, it was then I decided she was not the girl for me I mean what would my mother think.

The next time I had to go into her shop I could see and hear the sniggers from the other girls, to be fair they were lovely people and Anna was very kind and helpful but with my immaturity I always felt nervous in their company and tried to avoid having to meet with her but thanks for the memories Anna.

At the start of the project a French company working under the banner of a British company. Stent/Soletanche came on site to construct a diaphragm wall which would eventually form the basement wall, up till now the traditional way to build this would be to excavate a big hole in the ground build the wall then backfill around the outside of the wall, the difference with this method is they cast the wall first, using a machine called a Hydrofraise* then dig out the middle and hey presto you have a basement wall.

*The Hydrofraise is a drilling machine powered by three down-the-hole motors with reverse mud circulation. During operation, the Hydrofraise has a heavy metal frame which serves as a guide. The frame has two cutter drums equipped with tungsten carbide-tipped cutters which rotate in opposite directions in order to break up the soils. A pump placed immediately above the drums evacuates the loosened soil which is carried to the surface by the drilling mud. The mud is continuously filtered to remove the suspended cuttings and then poured back into the trench. The Hydrofraise assembly is mounted on a heavy crawler crane which carries the hydraulic power unit. The hydraulic power output is transmitted to the three down-the-hole motors, two of them driving the cutter drums and the third one operating the circulation pump. The hydraulic system is designed to provide the two cutter drums with a high torque at a low rotational speed. The guide frame is suspended from the crane hoist by a hydraulic ram which can be controlled either to provide a constant advance rate or to maintain a constant weight on the cutter drums (the maximum attainable being weight of the Hydro fraise I-e 25 tons for the HF 4000 and 60 tons for the HF 12000)

Standard excavation depth........................60m
Maximum excavation depth.......................150m
Cutter diameter ....1200 - 1400 mm
Maximum cutter torque at 300 bars.............4000 - 12000m.kg
Rotation motors power output....................110-330 HP
Circulation pump flowrate 450 m3/h
Maximum outlet pressure ....4.5 bars
Cutting tool total operating weight.............25-60 tons
Power-pack output at 1800 rpm................475-750 HP

A special feature of the Hydrofraise is that the cutting tool is capable of penetrating the concrete of a panel that has already set, to a thickness of several centimetres. Itis therefore possible to achieve good joints without using stop-ends when carrying out the construction of alternate panels. Another important advantage is that the drilling mud is constantly screened and desanded during excavation, thereby permitting reinforcement to be placed and concreting to be carried out as soon as the required depth has been reached

The crew building the wall were French and as there was only a three staff members from Wimpey as the junior member I was given the task of monitoring their work and progress, they pulled a 12hr shift which was fine I didn't mind the bit of overtime but my last task at the end of the day was to secure the site after they had left and there lay the problem, it could be anything up to 2hrs before they would leave the site so one evening I decided enough is enough and went into their office "Lad's, come on now you have to clear the site, I'm locking up in 10 minutes", my little speech was just met with cheers, laughter and a clinking of glasses, one of the lads had very good English, "Jon, Jon, you come sit down" so I just thought if you can't beat them join them, I sat and they poured me a shot of Pernod, "Do you want it neat" they asked "Err, have you any lemonade" I asked, next thing I knew all the heads turned in my direction and the driver of the Hydrofraise a very big guy with very little English, banged his fist on the table and went off on a rant of which I understood none but at the same time I did understand I had just insulted the way you should drink Pernod, I notice they were adding water and sheepishly I asked for water and the electric kettle was pushed in front of me, I found it a lovely way to take the drink and from that day on if I ever have Pernod I take it with water.

It was a great experience spending time with these guys, they had worked all over the world and whilst on this job, if something broke the right thing to do would be to order a new part, but because of some of the remote countries they worked in, countries where the nearest phone could be a 2-day drive, so these guys where a bit like the A Team, if something broke they took it apart, if they had a spare they replaced it, if they didn't then they made it, if they couldn't make it they figured out a way to circum vent it, they all had different skills, a fabricator, an electrician, an engineer etc.
Even when it came to their Pernod, they told me the story of running out of their precious retained French memory, they were working in Africa and still with several weeks before they would fly home they ran out of their elixir of life, the thought of several weeks without it was not an option, one of the guys travelled to the nearest hospital and after paying what locally was considered a large sum of money, well actually a bribe, to them it was less than a day's pay he returned with three 5 liter containers of medical alcohol, as this was a more pure form of alcohol it was watered down and an aniseed flavoring made from scratch added to complete the finished product, I remember the Hydro driver making a face, pretending to

spit the drink out saying "It was GOOD" in a loud booming voice followed by a similar laugh and much back slapping, I remember been happy that I was not in arms reach of this big man's back slaps, he was a giant.

At evening time, they played the same tape every night until the bottle was finished Free bird by Lynyrd Skynyrd, even though I heard it so often I never tired of it and still love it today.

They used to go home once a month and you didn't need a calendar to know when it was time for them to go home, the big fella who drove the Hydrofraise would start to get very grumpy as he missed his snuggles with his wife, they were a great crew and I enjoyed my time with them.

One day we got a call from a business quite close to the site, "Our basement has flooded, what are you people doing" this just didn't make sense to me, this shop was 100m along the shopping parade, no water had come out of the site so how could we be at fault, anyway Harry Hunt the project manager sent me off to investigate, I got to the shop to be met by a very irate shop owner, he told me to follow him into the basement and my heart jumped up in my chest, the basement was flooded to about a depth of four or five feet, boxes of chocolate bars, an ice cream fridge, shelving they were all floating around but not in water, it was Bentonite, the clay fluid we use on the site, not only was it bentonite but mixed in it was raw sewerage, it turns out that we had cut through a sewer pipe that did not appear on any drawings, it was not the only phone call we got as the day moved on more and more business's called the office.

The local paper The Coventry Evening Telegraph ran the incident on the front page, they had a field day with it getting all the stories from the disgruntled shop owners.

The contracts manager was on site the next day, newspaper in hand "I don't care what it takes, turn this around" slamming the copy on my desk, I had to meet all the parties involved and access each claim one by one with our insurance assessor, then I had an idea, one of the disgruntled parties was a young pop group, I met up with the lads and the following day took them to a local music shop where I had arranged to meet the local paper's photographer, the youngsters were just like kids in a sweet shop as they tried out the instruments and picked out new amps and equipment, I had previously contacted a bar in the city centre and arranged a gig with ourselves covering the cost off the band, the publicity worked a treat, the pub had a great night the band had a great night with pictures of them in bright yellow Wimpey T-shirts in the paper the next evening, under the headline City Contractor Saves the Day, the next morning whilst sitting at my desk I suddenly felt a bang on my hard hat, I spun around only to see the contracts manager walking out "Well done young un" That was about as good as it got from that man, I did fall foul of the newspaper some months later.

We had started work on the steel and glass dome that would be the crowning glory on this shopping centre, it was, at the time the biggest steel/glass dome in Europe and I got a phone call from the local rag "Can we send a photographer over to take some pictures".

He turns up and I'm told to give him the tour, so off we go him clicking away with his camera, we got to the top section and the steel glass dome, "This is incredible," he said, "it's amazing how you built it", he was doing this throughout the visit "Not really" I reply "It's just like a giant sized Meccano set, we bolt the sections together on the ground then offer it up into position using the cranes", "Oh you make it sound so easy" says the photographer and then it happened I put my size nines not only into my mouth but rammed them down my throat, "Well it was a bit windy on the day but apart from that we managed fine", I mean he's just a photographer what could happen.

Well this happened, Coventry Evening Telegraph headline the next day 'ENGINEERING FEAT COMPLETED IN THE HEART OF COVENTRY IN GAIL FORCE WINDS'

I got to work the next morning only to be met by 3 irate crane drivers, who's cranes had been shut down by the Factory inspector whilst they analysed the data recorders to see if the cranes had been working in winds above their safety limits, with the cranes shut down, the site basically ground to a halt and as the workers were paid by a production bonus I was hurting every workers pocket, I just about made it into the office only to be met by other members of staff "Nice knowing you Jon, we'll miss you when your gone"

I went into Harry Hunt's office "Jon, you've single handily managed to close down a multimillion pound project" Harry never raised his voice but he could give you the biggest rollicking of your life and scream at you without an increase of 1Db. "Harry, I never said that, all I said was it was a bit of a windy day", As I completed my sentence and Harry buried his head in his hands, eventually the cranes were cleared to operate and I just had to suffer 2 weeks of abuse before it died a death.

The Dome, many months later was to play a part in another memory I have on this contract, somebody planted a skull and bones pirate flag on top of the dome, I was walking past Harry's office when he called me in "Jon will you go up and remove that flag from dome".

On top of the dome was what they called a maintenance ladder, a steel ladder that went from the bottom to the top of the dome following the dome's curvature. By turning a handle, the steel ladder would go around the dome on a rail, so I set off up the ladder, I had just reached the top when I heard this distant really deep drone, I turned looking back wondering what it was, louder and louder, you could feel the vibrations coming through the ladder, then 2 dark spec's appeared in the distance, all of a sudden it made sense I had heard this noise before it was the unmistakable sound of a Merlin Engine, the 2 dark specs got closer and closer, it was a Spitfire and a Hurricane aircraft flying low over the city in a practise flight for a display that weekend marking the 50th anniversary of the battle of Britain and the bombing of Coventry.

There I was with the best seat in the house as these 2 incredible aircraft passed right over me maybe just a hundred feet above me, the noise was so loud and frightening yet exhilarating to the point where I had goose bumps all over my body, it was many many years before the camera phone would come into use so the only record I have of the event is my memory but I will never forget the awesome sound coming from those two engines.

The client of the project hired a publicity company to publicise the new shopping complex and one of their smart ideas was to have a countdown to the opening displayed on the side of the building and so it began at 100 DAYS TO OPENING, I couldn't believe it 100 days, just over 14 weeks we were a long way from finishing. We started a second shift, a night shift and guess who drew the short straw to supervise, of course it was yours truly.

The weeks were flying but the second shift was helping and we could see daylight, excuse the pun, with about 2 weeks to go shop fitters were setting up the shops, escalators and lifts were going, the lighting was nearing an end and the centre piece in the atrium a water feature using fibre optic cable was nearing completion, I had a very different relationship with the building than anyone else was ever going to have, all lit up at night including the glass dome and not a soul to be heard or seen, eventually we were down to the final week, there was still little items cropping up daily, lifts playing up, lights not working etc. By this time, I was not going home, I rented a room in a Bed and Breakfast, I never actually slept in the bed I would go over each day shower, change clothes and have a dirty big fried breakfast.

At quiet moment I got a few hours' sleep in my office, then it arrived, the day of the opening, I was on the fourth floor carpark making sure the white line's for the parking spaces were completed.

We could hear a brass band bursting into life as the shopping centre was opened, after three and a half years working on the job we opened up about 14 seconds after finishing the last carpark line.

I was exhausted, I couldn't even be bothered in going to the festivities, I went back into the office where I found Harry Hunt looking out the window of his office, I walked in "Harry, how come you're not down at the party", he turned around "Nah that's a job for the top brass" we chatted for a while a little bit of reminiscing and how he wanted ten more years then retire.

"How much leave do they owe you", "8 weeks" I answered back, Harry looked up at me "Then F##ck off out of here and I'll see you in a couple of months".

I headed off home, booked a flight over to America to visit my brother, I spent a month over there eating BBQ and playing golf, I travelled home to find one letter amongst my pile of unopened mail had the Wimpey Construction logo on it, I opened it thinking it would be telling me what project I was been move too only to find it was one of those letters that started Dear John, it is with regret blah blah blah, I was to be made redundant, I went to the site office in Coventry, knocked on Harry Hunt's door, Harry looked up from his desk, for a moment there was a smile then it disappeared "Come in Jon, take a seat", Harry went on to explain he fought the decision to let me go but that it was out of his hands, the industry was in trouble, it wasn't just Wimpey. When a ship's sinking it doesn't really lift the spirits when your told you're not the only one drowning. I was supposed to work on another month but Harry said I could leave when I wanted to so I cleared out my desk said nothing to anyone and slipped out the door.

As I walked down the stairs Anna spotted me and dashed over "Sweet heart, how are you, did you have a great holiday", I smiled "It was fabulous" with a stiff upper lip, but she read straight through me, "Jon, what's wrong", I went on to tell her what had happened, after a 20 second tirade of expletives, she just gave me a hug, "Are you going today", "yes" I replied, she gave me a hug and a big kiss on the cheek which when I got in the car I spotted the remains of the lipstick, "Promise you'll come visit us", I smiled, "of course I will", I got in to my car, drove home and never saw them again.

CH12
In England, I'm a plastic Paddy, in Ireland, I'm an English man

After getting laid off from Wimpey construction I decided to head to Galway and see my folks, it was 1992, my father was not the type of guy that thought the world owed him a living, he worked for everything he got and even in retirement it didn't change, I booked the car ferry with a return date in a month's time, I arrived looking forward to a nice long rest and moms own cooking, I don't think dad actually said hello, his first words were "I've a number of jobs that I saw in the paper, I've torn the adds out and I've sent off for application forms from some of the local contractors", so my month of lounging around lasted less than 5 minutes, before I even got a cup of tea I was filling out job applications.

There was one special moment that I still treasure today, it was the day I saw my Dad cry for the first time, my giant, my mentor, my hero sat in his chair wiping tears from his eyes, I had seen him bury his mother, his Sister, his Brothers but there he sat crying.... WHY...? It was because his beloved Donegal had just beat Dublin in the all-Ireland final of 1992 and they proudly held the Sam McGuire trophy aloft in victory, the first time Donegal had won the trophy, my dad wiped the tears saying he never thought he would see it in his lifetime buy twenty years on in 2012 I he watched once more as Donegal beat Mayo and became All Ireland champions again and I cherish the memory of been with him watching the game.

Before I knew it, the month was gone, it just flew by, only seemed like 4 weeks but just before I headed home I got an interview with Dublin Corporation, the boat was due off at 3.00pm and my interview was at 11.00am.

I found the Corporation office and was sent up to the fourth floor where I was seated with 4 other candidates, I remember thinking they looked so much more business-like than I was, I was satisfied with the interview and off I headed back to Blighty and back to bills and council poll tax.

Less than a week passed and I got a letter telling me I was successful in my application and they offered me the position of clerk of works.

The Institute of Clerk of Works

The role of Clerk of Works is one of the most important positions in the construction industry. The Clerk of Works role is to monitor quality of work, check and supervise all construction details, record progress, and generally be the eyes and ears of the client and is seconded to the design team for reporting purposes.

I was overjoyed, my spell as an unemployed statistic was over.

When I got there the project I was to start on had been delayed so they put me into the housing department, my first role was monitoring contractors works on upgrades to corporation properties, I was sent out with this chap called Jim, Jim was a Quantity Surveyor and a very well dressed and spoke with a rather posh accent so I was surprised when we got to his car it was a really battered Nissan that had seen much better days but this first day with Jim served as a lesson I would never forget.

We arrived at a place called Ballyfermot, I was very green and knew nothing of the different area's around Dublin.

We arrived and parked up in the estate and waited for the contractor to arrive, Jim was reading notes on the job whilst I just sat watching the world pass by then BANG a large stone bounced of the front screen, I jumped up in surprise "F##k Me" I shouted, I looked over Jim hadn't even broke his gaze on the paperwork, all of a sudden I could hear kids screaming "Ya f##cking w##kers", I was sitting bolt upright in the seat, another stone bounced off the bonnet hitting the windscreen, Jim still hadn't moved, not even a flinch "Jesus Jim are you not going to do anything" I yelled, Jim broke off from his reading, glanced over and said "they'll soon get bored", the kids kept up the abuse eventually Jim finished reading put his papers back in his case, "Jon" he said "If we get out and give chase they will disappear through some garden or back alley and by the time we get back to the car there won't be a nut or a bolt left on it, live and learn.

I went one day to the Ballymun flats, made famous in the movie 'Into the West', I was with a contractor on about the fourth floor, we were out on the balcony when the contractor looked down to see 3 youths pulling at items he had in the back of his pickup truck, he screamed at them to stop only to receive a torrent of abuse back and laughter, those men knew it would take him 4 to 5 minutes to get down to the ground floor and by that time they would have sorted out what to take and what to leave, the last of the Ballymun flats were demolished in 2016 to tears and cheers from the local residents, some folk mourned the loss of a home that went back a number of generations whilst others cheered the death of drug fuelled menagerie.

Dublin is divided in half by the river Liffey and so this gives you the North-siders and the South-siders two very distinctly different groups, the north is considered the working class and the south the upper class.

I remember watching Shamrock Rovers football fans after attending a game against Bohemians FC at Dalymount park crossing the O'Connell bridge over the Liffey then getting down on their hands and knees and kissing the Ground, so ingrained was the North-South divide.

Eventually the contract I was originally engaged for commenced it was called 'The Tara Street Control and Command centre', the idea was to have all 999 calls come to one centre of operations this would allow a greater knowledge and control of Emergency services across the City and County, for example if both fire tenders were out on duty from Phibsborough fire station and another call came from the Phibsborough area a tender from the nearest station would be sent to the emergency.

I turned up to work and was introduced to the site agent, a man called John Doherty, a good Donegal name and he of course recognising my name as coming from Donegal there was an instant bond between us.

Ireland were in the qualifiers for the 1994 world cup in the USA, the project had been going about 9 months when one day John stuck his head around my office door, "Are you coming down the pub to watch the match", at this time Lansdowne Road where Ireland played their home matches did not have flood lights and hence their games were played at 2.00pm, "John" I replied "We can't both go down, there has to be a senior member of management remain on the site in case of any problems". Well spoken, I thought to myself quite pleased at my managerial tone, "There won't be any problems Johnny, all the lads have gone down" "What?" Says I "you can't just close the site", "Oh no Johnny, we're not closing the site, we tried that once, we tried locking them in and they just climbed over the gates, so are you ready?" Again it was something that took a while to get used to, down I went to the pub, a big roar rang out as myself and john entered the and a seat kept for us with a pint in front of it, it was just like the French lads in Coventry all over again don't try fixing something just because you think you have to, give the lads some understanding let them enjoy the games and get it back tenfold when needed, I would write all about the craic we had during those games but if I'm honest I don't remember much of it.

We got taken out a few times by Columba Bonner an Uncle of Paki Bonner the Celtic and Irish goalkeeper, Columba was a sub-contractor on the site, I know it was wrong and I'm not condoning it but Columba would take us home in his Jag after maybe a 10-hour stint on the beer, he drove up a one-way street in Dublin, next thing we could see the blue light, the cops stopped us got out Columba put the window down and the cop sticks his head in "Sure how ya Columba, jaysus, some game today, what" and then we would be on our way, John was taking me home one night and we got lost so we just pulled over to the side of the road and went to sleep, the next morning everything looked so much clearer.

It was a crazy time but I would not change one day it was a great experience, we had a few more crazy days out during qualification a 1-1 draw with Northern Ireland meant second place in the group and automatic qualification, I was watching this last game in The Blanchardstown Inn, Dublin 15, I remember women screaming, cheering hugging, going crazy as Ireland qualified, these same women six months earlier thought a sweeper was something you used to clean the backyard, now everyone was an expert.

Suddenly the pub as one broke into song…. Neil Diamond's America.

Ask an Irishman where he was when Armstrong landed on the moon, he probably won't remember, ask him where he was when

Ray Houghton scored against Italy and he'll know precisely where he was, I was in Coyne's Tavern in Galway, sitting in the bar, pint in hand wandering if there was any way Ireland could hold this Italian team to a nil - nil draw then Ray Houghton pops one in from 25 yards it caught the whole pub by surprise it may only have been a milli second but it was there that small moment of disbelief then YEAAAAAAAAA.

The Tara street job was in full swing and although as a clerk of works your supposed to keep a professional relationship with the contractor I couldn't help but become good friends with John Doherty, he was a very clever man who had a habit of putting his foot in his mouth.

I was in a meeting in my office with the senior Engineer for the project when there was a loud knock on the door, suddenly john's head appeared around the door "Sorry to interrupt but I thought I'd better let you know the IRA are on their way they'll be here after lunch" the door closed and myself and the Engineer stared at the door in disbelief at what we just heard only for the door to open again "Sorry" said john "I meant The IDA will be here after lunch"

IDA Ireland's main objective is to encourage investment into **Ireland** by foreign owned companies. It works as a strategic partner and provides consultancy and support services to Irish companies, home and abroad.

At site meetings we had a structural engineer and a Mechanical engineer who both had stutters and please I'm not mocking this it's a terrible affliction, but the two men might be arguing a point and their stutters would become more pronounced and you could see

John leaning towards the men his mouth forming to say a word, then he would say it and it would inevitably be wrong then the engineer would get frustrated "NNNo thththats nnnot whwhwhat I mmmeant", I couldn't stay quiet "John will you be quiet and give them a chance", "ohh right Johnny, ok Johnny", they were the longest site meetings I ever had to attend.

It was coming to the end of the contract and the painters were in, John introduced me to their Forman, a man by the name of Nesty, he was a man in his 60's who suffered an obvious spinal curvature disorder. congenital kyphosis

"So Johnny, this is the painting Foreman Nesty, I've been on a number of jobs with him, a very tasty painter, great at skirting boards", Nesty looked up from his bent position "f##k you, you Donegal Pr##k".

At this stage in my life I was living in Blanchardstown and it was a town because today it's been engulfed by what can only be described as Greater Dublin.

I used to take a pint in the Blanchard's town inn and although one or two people turned when they heard my English accent on the whole they were very friendly and accommodating.

In 1994 Dublin reached the All Ireland final, they had not won the Sam McGuire Trophy since 1983 when they beat Galway by 2 points in front of a 72,000 crowd well whatever the crowd was to be for the 1994 final it would be one person short.

I didn't really know many people in the pub, one or two would put their hand up and say hello, but one chap called Mick, whom I never seen in any other shirt than a Dublin shirt would always give me a wave and a how ya. A week before the final mick came into the bar a bit worst for drink but cheering and shouting, when his pals got him to quieten down Mick produced his All Ireland finals ticket and showed it to anybody that would look.

Sunday came, I thought I'd watch the game in the pub for the atmosphere, I got there maybe 10 mins into the game, bought a pint then looked for a spot with a view of the TV, I thought I saw a bench seat free but as I got close to it I noticed somebody curled up having a kip, it was a blue Dublin shirt covering the man and as I looked up at the face, it was Mick.

I felt sorry for the guy and a bit angry that someone did not wake him and let him off to the match, as it happened Dublin were unsuccessful and lost by 2 points to County Down.

After the game was over I was chatting to a lad next to me, I voiced my opinion on poor old Mick missing the game and the fact that no one woke him but the lad said "Had we woke him and sent him on his way, the chances were he would be passed out somewhere no ticket, no money at least here we can keep an eye on him here and he'll get home tonight" I realized how right he was and yes there are scum bags living north and south in Dublin but the true north sider is a very friendly accommodating character.

My next job in Dublin was to be a roof restoration to city hall, Dame street in the heart of the city.

I have to say if you ever find yourself on Dame street pop into city hall the Atrium area where you can look up into the dome, it shows some wonderful architecture finished off with incredible artwork, it was also the place where the first meeting of the new independent Irish government was held after the uprising.

I was working with an Architect from the Corporation by the name of Ronan Boylan, he was one of those strange creatures that tried to be Eccentric but couldn't afford it, he always dressed in a dickie bow and always surrounded himself at meetings with those who he thought would have the right answers, he never wanted to find himself been put on the spot, so much so that a meeting he called in the city center regarding one of the old fountains, so many people turned up at his request that the Gaurdi arrived to break up what they thought was a protest.

We were in the Hugh Lane gallery one day looking at replacing some of the rotten window frames, as we walked through a room Ronan spotted that one of the cherub statues in the room had been defaced, he gave a 'tut' and carried on, a security guard came towards us and Ronan stopped him, "That cherub on the left as we look has had its Gena Talia defaced with a marker pen", the guard carried on stood in front of the statue and began scratching his head, Ronan shouted across the room "The genitals man, the genitals", the guard still scratching his head, turned and shrugged his shoulders, Ronan pulled off his cap hitting it against his thighs and shouted "His cock you fool, look at his cock",

The job on city hall was to remove the lead on the roof and return it back to a copper roof, as the way it had been originally built, it was interesting work as it incorporated a skill that would rarely be seen these days.

We had been on the job about 6 weeks when Ronan called one of his site meetings on the roof, about 8 officials from the corporation gathered on top all listening to Ronan about how the job was going, what stages it would be broken into and all of a sudden I realized he was repeating exactly what I had told him some 40 minutes earlier, the crafty little fecker, I had to explain half of it to him like I was talking to a three-year-old yet there he stood sure of everything he said.

"Ronan, how long is it since the roof was last done" asked one of the corporation staff assembled, "Hmm" said Ronan, looking across at me for a hint of an answer "I would think it about 50 years ago" answered Ronan "56 years ago" came this voice, everyone turned in unison to see where it came from but no one was there or so it seemed then Pat the chief copper smith got off his hands and knees "56 years ago" He repeated, Ronan stood opened mouth, "And how would you know that", Pat looked at Ronan "Because I worked on it, I was a thirteen year old apprentice when it was re-roofed", he picked up some tools and walked away, Ronan just stood there aghast.

Pat had his son Brendan working on the job with him and always referred to him as the 'Young'un' even though Brendan was 53 years' old.

Pat could take a single sheet of copper and make it move in several different directions without cutting into it, I was discussing the skill of Pat with his son Brendan who told me his father would come to a tricky bit of work, he would ask Brendan to fetch something for him and when he'd get back Pat would have the tricky bit done and Brendan would be none the wiser on how he did it, Brendan would complain but Pat would roll out the same response "When I think your good enough young'un I'll teach you".

Pat was at retirement age and would turn up to work at about 10.00 am, he had to climb four 25 foot ladders in order to reach the roof, all personal used to descend the ladders for breakfast break and lunch, not paddy, once he climbed up he stayed up there until finishing at 5.00pm.

I've never had any aspirations to enter into politics whether local or national, so my eye's where opened at what I witnessed in City Hall.

When work was ongoing on the roof and the council was meeting, I used to sit in the public gallery, mobile phone in hand and monitor the noise levels, I was taken back at the tactics used by the different parties, trying to gain one up man ship on their counterparts, a councilor stood up and read a report regarding a recent trip to Glencolmcille for 6 councilors attending the Irish college, for obvious reasons my ears pricked up on hearing Glen been mentioned, he gave a glowing report on the college informing the other councilors of the type of work the college was doing in order to try and keep the language alive and teach it to a new generation, about 4 hrs. earlier that day I was in one of the City Hall offices discussing the works programme with some staff managers and had overheard one of the girls telling her work colleague how she had to accompany the Councilor's on their trip to Donegal, she had to attend all the lectures, take notes then prepare the very speech that was been read out in the chamber, whilst the Councilor's spent each and every day they were up there on the Golf course.

Another day I was doing the same thing in the council chamber, just monitoring the noise, I was sat at the back of the public gallery and out of view from most of the councilor's, they were discussing, travel allowance and other allowances and payments to councilor's, they started to vote on how much these allowances would be raised for the start of 1996, all of a sudden one of the councilor's spotted me, he suddenly rose to his feet "Point of order Mr. Chairman but this is a closed meeting yet there is someone sitting in the public gallery, can I ask that he is ejected immediately", at once all councilor's heads turned in my direction "What are you doing there?" asked the chairman "and what are you writing down", the level of murmuring rose as all members awaited my response, I told him who I was and what I was doing and said I was there at the direct request of the city manager, blah, blah, blahhhh.

Heads turned and mumbling increased, then the chairman asked me to leave and so I did and those poor plastic politicians voted in their payments for the year.

I had been taking progress photos with a real camera as the Iphone was still many years away from been invented and as it was getting close to lunch time instead of going into my office I set off in search of my lunch from one of the local shops, I was walking down Dame street and was about 100m from the AIB Bank on the corner of Dame street and Palace Street, all hell broke loose at first I had no idea what was going on, then as screaming pedestrians ran passed me, I realized a bank raid was in progress. A car was parked adjacent to where I was walking at that moment I was not aware that it was the getaway car and an unmarked car came screeching up in an attempt to block any attempt of the gangsters car pulling off but it over shot and ended up on the pavement pedestrians pushed past me as I took my camera out and started taking photos, the unmarked car reversed back to block the getaway car but the officer in the passenger seat had opened his door and as the driver reversed back the door was torn from its hinges at the same time as this was going on a plain clothes officer wearing a corporation jacket reached into his road sweeping handcart and pulled out an automatic weapon aimed and pointed it at the car screaming at the occupants to remain still, I carried on clicking away taking photos of the car and the bank by this time most of the public had fled the scene and I realized I was standing between heavily armed police officers and heavily armed gangsters, it was then that my bottom started trembling, I stopped taking photos and carefully retraced my steps back towards my office, just then I heard shouting, I turned to see a number of officers pointing a gun at a suspect who was lying down on the ground, I found out later that this man was a member of the gang and as he came out of the bank he quickly realized that it was an ambush and the cops were waiting for them and ten out of ten for quick thinking this man joined the queue for the Cash machine, but his downfall came when one of the bank employees came outside and recognized him as one of the robbers.

Safe in my office I started to go through in my mind just what had happened, it was like a dream, the site agent on the job came into my office and I started to relay what had just occurred, the nerves in my voice, I must have sounded like a six-year-old telling his father what had happened at school, "Then he pulled out a gun, then reverse, bang the door was gone" eventually I calmed down and started to think about what I had on my camera, my first thought was to contact one of the red tops but the Sun and the Mirror where not printed in Ireland at this time, The Daily Star was the only red top printed here, so I gave them a call, I asked if they had heard about the robbery and that I had photos of the event, they sent a taxi to pick me up and take me over to their office where I received a tour of the place whilst they took my camera off for developing, I have to say it was very interesting, it was that era where digital was coming in but was not fully functional and some of the historical ways of producing a paper were still been practiced.

The next day the story was in The Star and they had used 2 of my photographs and about three days later I got a cheque for £100.00 just about half my weekly wage, myself and my wife had a wonderful night out with food and drink all courtesy of a 35mm film clip.

On the roof on city hall were about 8 chimney stacks, each stack had an outlet for 6 fireplaces, the brickwork on most of the stacks needed attention but before we could work on them we had to trace them to see which rooms were attached to each stack, you could generalize which fireplaces used which chimney but there was no way of knowing which of the six individual stacks were then attached to that fireplace, so we bought some smoke bombs, just light the bomb leave it in the fire grate and someone on top marked which pot the smoke was coming out, a simple enough solution to a small problem, that was until one day, I was in one of the office's that was used by about twenty staff members, the room had two fireplaces, I lit the smoke bomb and this caused a bit of banter amongst the staff, it was a distraction from their usual daily routine, "Is that dangerous?", "Is that poisonous?" the staff were shouting over at me, I had so many remarks I could have hit back with but thought better if I kept my gob shut, I reached the second fireplace, put the bomb at the rear of the fire surround and lit it, within seconds it was obvious something was wrong, there was no draw on the smoke the fireplace filled with smoke, then it started billowing into the room, we later found out the flue had been blocked up, some of the girls spotted it and started girly screaming (that's going to cost me) it then snowballed into complete panic, somebody screamed "Its poisoness don't breathe it". I was on my hands and knees in front of the fireplace, "It's not poisiness, look, look" and I started taking in big breath's of the smoke like some demented eejit, but it did nothing to quell the panic.

I ended up in front of the city manager, I was with Ronan Boylan the Architect for the project, the manager asked me what had happened "Well sir, we were" I did not have my sentence finished when Ronan interrupted me, "You do not address the Manager as sir, you address him as Manager", I couldn't resist it "Sorry Mr. Manager, begging your pardon", Ronan started turning purple, you could see the veins rising at his forehead "It's not Mr. Manager, it's just Manager" Ronan was looking straight at me, visible shaking, all this time the Manager had not broken his gaze from some documents he had in front of him, "John, just make sure this sort of thing doesn't happen again" "Yes sir" I responded, turned on my heel and out his door.

CH 13
BYE BYE DUBLIN, HELLO GALWAY

My time with Dublin Corporation came to an end, I had spotted a job offer in Galway, had the interview and was offered the job.

The contract was The Tuam Rural Water scheme, I won't bore you with details of this job.

This contract was coming to an end after nearly three years so I studied the newspapers looking to see what was available and I spotted, applied for and got a technician grade job on the Donegal town bypass.

This was a great contract with some really good work colleagues, one day I was out with Michael McGarvey, one of the Resident Engineers, we were driving the route of the bypass, at this time the ground works had only just begun so we were driving across fields in an Isuzu Jeep, we had a number of these vehicles for the RE (Resident Engineer) staff, as vehicles they were probably fine on the road nice and comfortable but as off road vehicles they were useless and we were forever having to get a tow out of the mud but back to this story, I was heading back towards the Site offices, Michael was making some notes on a drawing not really paying attention to the route I was taking, we were heading down a hill and got to a section that had been traversed by the big Volvo dump trucks, over the days their wheels had cut a deep trench into the topsoil, I hit one of these tracks then another, Michael was thrown forward his head hitting the dash board, thrown back into his seat then repeated once more as I hit the second track, I stopped looked over, Michael was looking down at his notes completely silent, "Did the air bag work" I said…… "F##k you yer bo####ks" was all that came back.

A few days later, the Senior Resident Engineer (SRE) came onto the site of the first bridge to be built, he was carrying a copy of the Donegal Democrat, the local paper, "How's the alignment of the bridge" he asked, this particular bridge was quite a tricky one, it crossed the river at an angle, in other words it wasn't perpendicular to the river, it also consisted of two arches that grew in width as they went up and across eventually joining together in the center splitting into 2 arches again as it crossed over the river, "Its fine" I replied "How fine" the SRE, enquired at the same time handing me the newspaper, 'New Bypass Bridge Constructed In The Wrong Place', it went on to read 'The first bridge to be constructed on the new bypass is said to be 3.00m out of position blah blah blah, I looked up at the SRE, "Well it's not 3.00m out of position" I replied, "But how far out is it? I need to call them". "Ok," I said give me an hour and I'll get back to you", myself and Michael headed off and an hour later I was standing outside the SRE's office, "Come in" he shouted after I tapped his door, "Well", he looked up at me, he had a smile on his face but it wasn't a nice friendly smile, more a sinister one "We've checked it 4 times" I said "And the largest error we can find is 2.4mm", his smile broadened, "That will do, thank you very much Jon". He enjoyed been right.

The SRE had a constant one up manship battle with the Contracts manager for Patton's, the main contractor, he sent a memo over complaining of site staff parking outside the RE staff's offices, he said he wanted a fence erected to distinguish the RE staff carpark from the general carpark, he was expecting a six-foot palisade fence or similar to be erected but instead the contractor fitted a fancy chain fence, about 18 inches high like something you would fit in your garden.

We had 4 Isuzu standard commercial style jeeps for use on the site and one 6 seater jeep for taking the top brass around when they called to site, it was the posh one, we always made sure it was kept clean inside and out.

One day there was a problem with a concrete delivery and I needed to go out to site but all the vehicles including the quad bikes were out, I went into Neil and asked for the keys to the 6 seater, he threw them to me saying "don't get it dirty", I was rushing as I wanted to check this load of concrete out as soon as possible, I pulled out, I could hear the stones, hitting the wheel arches as the wheels spun in the gravel but then BANG followed by a horrible scraping sound "Oh shit" I said loud, I stopped got out and checked, I had caught one of the steel post's on our fancy garden fence, it had caught the back of the wheel arch ripped through the wing and down the passenger door, I wasn't up to my neck in shit, it was past my ears.

I went over to the concrete delivery, got everything sorted there then headed back to the site offices wondering how I was going to explain several thousand-euro's worth of damage to the jeep.

There was no point putting it off, as soon as I got back to the carpark I was knocking on Neil's door and he shouted "Enter", I stepped inside, I went to speak, "Err, err, err" Neil looked up "What's up" "Oh shit" I replied "there is no way I can dress it up, I caught the carpark fence post with the 6 seater and ripped a big hole down the side of it", I waited for the rollicking of a lifetime but instead Neil's fist banged on his desk and he burst out laughing, "I told them, I told them it was too fecking low, I didn't want to laugh but you know the way its infectious and couldn't help it a smile came on my face but I fought back and presented a look of concern to Neil, "Well that's going to cost them a few bob to put right", I just replied "I'm sorry Neil it was just an accident", "Oh don't worry about it Jon, if they had built a proper fence it wouldn't have happened", I just thought, good enough and walked out amazed that I was free from blame.

I tended to work on my own and did not use the jeeps, we also had a Peugeot 205 van which I could get to all the bridge sites but at times I needed to travel the bypass route which at this stage in the contract was a muddy mess due to the big Volvo A20's, these are the big dump trucks with the 6-foot-high wheels, so in places the mud could be 2 to 3-foot deep, so back to the quad bike, I was heading up the cut when I came on 4 lads walking the route back to their machines as I reached them I pulled up and we had the crack for a few minutes, I was just about to head off when Declan asked me for a lift, we had been told that we were not to give lifts, an insurance thing, so I said no, "Jesus Jon don't be such a miserable ass" said Declan as he clambered on the back, I didn't argue and started to pull away slowly "Jump on" says Declan and before I knew it I had three more lads on the quad, one behind Declan, then another lad behind him on the rear carry frame and to finish it off one lad on the front carry frame, all in all five of us on a single quad bike. Gingerly I accelerated slowly and started to move away then Declan put his hand over mine and held down the accelerator on full and all of a sudden we took off, I'm sure the screams could be heard all over the county, after a few bad bumps we lost the lad on the rear carrier and still Declan held my thumb hard down on the throttle, we were hitting some big ruts and the ride even with the nice padded seat I had was becoming very uncomfortable for me but for the poor lad on the front metal carrier it was agony and he was screaming at the top of his voice to stop, eventually I got control back of the throttle and came to a stop but it was a bit too late for the lad on the front carrier who damaged his coccyx and was off work for 6 weeks, I never asked what they wrote in the accident book.

CH 14

QUEST.

NOUN

1. a long or arduous search for something:

"the quest for a reliable vaccine has intensified"

synonyms: search · hunt · pursuit · pursuance of · investigation into something or someone.

A few years back this was a word very rarely used in general conversation, but now days' computer games have given it a whole new lease of life.

To me it means something very different, Hope, Success and understanding.

Quest is the name of the Brain injury service in Galway, who's programme helped me come to terms with my brain injury.

Myself and Claire went in and I had an interview while they explained their services to me, to be honest when I came out I actually had no clue as what they could do for me and I wondered if it was for me, I told Claire I would give it 5 weeks, "Would that be fair" I asked and Claire said yes, two years later they nearly had to push me out of the place. I quickly realised that there is no single plan that covers brain injury as there is no such thing as two brain injuries the same but their experience allowed them to formulate a program that fitted me and the biggest part of the program was giving me an understanding of my injury.

I met some wonderful people in there, people who I would not have normally associated with and by that I mean folk 30 years younger than me, at breakfast and lunch time there is a single large table where we all sit and it doesn't matter if you are the President of Ireland or a hooker, we are all at the same level because we all have a brain injury. (there are no hookers attending, maybe I should have used a different example)

The staff there were very experienced and kind (oh my god, you can't imagine how hard that was to type) although they did have very definite personalities themselves isn't that right Mr. Grumpy, Miss I'm so pretty, the intelligent one and the one from Mayo…

Please excuse me going off on a tangent all the other staff were lovely.

It had an element of the NRH about it because for example those with good mobility would help those less mobile, it had the same camaraderie.

I still call in to their office now and again, despite them changing the access code on the door.

I think most people who have passed through the doors of Quest will have found the experience a very positive one, so I would like to thank all the staff and clients of Quest and dedicate this book to my dogs Charlie and Gracie, (well I do have a brain injury).

Croi have also been of great service to me and my PA Stephanie from the wheelchair Association, without these people my life would be very different, maybe living on the French Riviera or Surfing in Hawaii…………….

CH 15
EVERYONE'S A ROCK STAR

2005 Was the height of the good times in Ireland where we all had money burning holes in our pockets, I remember a lad who was qualified as an electrician persuading a bank to lend him 1.75 million Euro for a housing development, it was around this time that we were looking for our purchase in Donegal, prior to buying the cottage we did look at 2 sites, one had permission for a 5 bed house the other had permission for 10 houses, all we did was make an enquiry but the guy we sat in front of said "No need to choose, you could go for both", he then went on to offer us an obscene amount of money with payment terms of an interest only loan, it was mad Ted, a low level Council worker and a nurse, I came out of the meeting shaking with shock, I would like to think I didn't go as crazy as some people bud I did get a wonderful present from Claire, she said she would pay for a week in a recording studio.

Now I had a number of songs I had written myself and started going through them to see which ones I would like to record, I wrote a couple of new ones and off I went into the recording studio, the first studio was Shay's Recording Studio, Kylebrack, Loughrea, Co. Galway, he was a small outfit but a very capable engineer, it was just me and my guitar, I then took what I had to Kenny Ralph, Sun

Street studios Tuam, he helped me enormously with his experience, he brought in a few more musicians and slowly my songs simmered in the oven of his mixing desk until they rose like a perfect soufflé.

Kenny is without doubt a great talent, he took the energy of The Saw Doctors and brought it to life on CD.

You become very attached and protective of your songs so it was great to have someone who understood that and would try and enhance your creation and not over take it.

I released the album in 2005 at The Tuam Earwig Arts festival and was taken back by its success, I also came up with a novel way of selling it, I used the Saw Doctor chat board, to bring it to the attention of their fans as the last track on the album was a live performance where I joined the band on stage during a fund raising gig for Paul Cunniffe's family, so on their chat board page I announced the CD and made a crazy offer, 'send me your address and I will send you the CD, promise to play it completely three times then if you like it, send me a tenner if you don't then use it as a Frisbee, out of the hundreds I sent off only one guy did not pay me but the cheeky fecker put it on Ebay and sold it for 15 pounds sterling.

I have listened to many a song without knowing the full meaning of them, I'll just show you what I mean.

You're so vain, Carly Simon…. " you probably think this song is about you." The title subject's identity has long been a matter of speculation, with Simon stating that the song refers to three men, only one of whom she has named publicly, actor Warren Beaty one of the others is rumored to be Mick Jagger, I'm not sure of the third.

Gary Brooker and Keith Reid wrote **Whiter Shade of pale** but it was Keith Reid who got the title and starting point for the song at a party. He overheard someone at the party saying to a woman, "You've turned a whiter shade of pale," and the phrase stuck in his mind.

The author of the book *Procol Harum: beyond the pale*, Claes Johansen, suggests that the song "deals in metaphorical form with a male/female relationship which after some negotiation ends in a sexual act."

Now I don't have a story to match anything like that but I will for the first time explain why and how I wrote the songs that ended up on my album.

Now for those of you who did not get the limited edition of my book, you will not have the free CD, so you may want to skip this chapter.

ALBUM TITLE- Time to go Lakes – This is a reference to a Tuam slang term, if you were at a mad house party you might say *"Ah man the party last night was Lakes"* or maybe someone gets a bit drunk *"Jaysus, ya should have seen him last night he was Lakes"*

Track. 1.- **World is getting smaller**--- This is very relevant today, some years back a man was taken hostage by the 'Taliban' they were going to execute him because he was American, he was shown on TV, on his knees, begging for his life.

It was found that he had an Irish connection and the Irish Media and public tried to put pressure on the Irish government to issue him with an Irish passport and claim him as an Irish citizen in the hope of getting him released, it didn't work, the man actually escaped his captures only to be recaptured and beheaded.

So this song was about how the evil in the world could reach out and touch anybody, no one and no place was safe.

Track. 2.- **It's Alright**--- This was about changing from childhood to adulthood, a lot of pressure is put on kids to do well in their exams and if you fail although your only 17 your life is over and you will amount to nothing…B##@@cks, I believe we all have a chance to find our niche in life, there is a line in it "Can't see the words upon the board", that was about me, I have never been tested but I'm sure I have a touch of dyslexia, if I'm put under pressure to read something quickly like subtitles on the TV I sometimes freeze on a word and just cannot get passed it….. Stop the pressure let people be what they want to be.

Track. 3. – **Time to go Lakes** – This is the title track, about the Tuam arts festival and as I explained earlier just time to have fun.

Track.4. – **Going Down to Glasgow** – Firstly this song has nothing to do with Glasgow, I needed a name of a place that rhymed with Shadow, you see it could be any town, any city, any place. I felt I had reached a crossroads in my own life, I was 45 years old, had a wonderful partner and needed to have substance in my life, settle down, stop playing the wanna be musician and start coming home at weekends before 3.00am, get my imaginary pipe and slippers, I'd been running since my teens it was time to slow down.

Track. 5. – **How Come** – On the original album after this title I wrote in brackets "small town syndrome, STS" because, and it's not just Tuam, there are a thousand small towns in Ireland just like it.

Its where everybody knows what you had for breakfast before you even dip your toast into the runny egg.

I had separated from my then wife and if I so much as looked at another woman in a pub or heaven forbid if I spoke to one of them by the time I've had my second piss there will be gossip about me somewhere in town, I was spoken to by a few not very happy husbands and me totally innocent (well mostly).

I suppose if truth be known at that stage I was a bit down in the dumps and feeling sorry for myself "If lightning strikes, it always aims for me". Because of my separation people who I thought were my friends would cross the road when they seen me, it was a lonely time and a small town just made it harder.

Track.6.- **Going home in the pouring rain** – Ahh now this track is auto biographical, it's about the first time I met Claire "Saw this name upon the screen it read, Indian for peace" Claire's email address was shamshanti which comes from Hindu and roughly translates as '*Peace and well-being*', we had met briefly one night and agreed to meet for a glass of wine the next day.

"didn't know what to expect that day, a bit of fun at least", I went to meet her in O Toole's Supermarket carpark, she pulled up in her car popped out and jumped into my jeep (a black Cherokee). She had blue jeans a light brown leather jacket and a cream cheese cloth blouse I remember thinking, Oh dear, she's a bit out of my league but I just thought what the heck we can head off and have a bit of fun.

Well I told you earlier about this song how Claire put me out on a really wet night and the following Thursday I persuaded her to call around to my flat

I said "Hey listen to this, I've been working on a new song", at that stage it wasn't complete but I reached the chorus "And now I'm going home in the pouring rain, pouring rain" and Claire burst into a fit of laughter, she knew straight away it was about her and if I'm honest I think that's when I knew I wanted to spend the rest of my life with her.

Track.7.- **Rock N Roll** – I always wanted to write a rock n roll song, you know that song the DJ puts on because the dance floor is empty and within seconds the floor is full, I wrote the first and second verse quite quickly then got stuck, I was sitting up in bed one Sunday morning when it came to me, I just borrowed a few lines or name's, from the greats i.e. When Buddy played for Peggy Sue and heart break hotel all's going well just down on Blueberry hill.

Track.8.- **Come on Down** – This song is all about life, not necessarily my life, but anybody's life, you have this stage in life where you are no longer a child and not really an adult or at least an adult with common sense, you may be working and have a few bob in your pocket, you throw your clothes in the corner of the room and magically they appear 3 days later in your wardrobe all nice and clean and pressed, responsibilities 0, fun 10.

There is a line in the song that goes like this 'I love the summer time there's a great stretch in the night, its 6am my friends and that's why it's so bright' that line came from a story told to me from a well-known native of Tuam, let's just call him john, we were having a drink one day and he told me of a night he met up with a friend one summers evening and they had a right good session, last ones to leave the pub about 1.30am, john said, "We'll have one last drink at the house" so off they went back to johns for a last tipple and so they have a few more drinks, then despite protestations john persuades his drinking companion to eventually go home as its 6.00am, he gathers the fella up by the arm out into the hallway opens the front door a beaming shaft of morning sunlight hits them in the face, yer man looks at john and says "Jaysus, isn't there a mighty stretch in the evening."

Track.9. **Hands of Time** – I'm not telling you about this song, somethings just need to stay buried so listen to it and take what you want from it, I do feel it's the best song I have ever written and I have a plan for it later on in the year…… so watch this space.

Track.10. – **My Selector** – I mentioned this earlier in the book, it's an old reggae song found by Paul Cunniffe and I played and sang on it along with the Saw Doctors

Music is still in my life I have ideas for songs but as yet, have done nothing about it, this bloody book really takes up a lot of time.

CH16

The Last Chapter

In hindsight, not the best name for a chapter, it makes it sound like I'm finished and believe me there could be nothing further from the truth, I lost 2 good friends this year as I realise I'm getting to that age but instead of mourning them it kicked me up the ass and said get out there McGinley and enjoy life, so as it was my wife's 50th birthday I decided to give her the holiday of a lifetime, and off we headed to Orlando and Las Vegas.

Orlando because Claire was a big fan of Harry Potter, reading the books way before a mention of a movie, so I had tickets purchased for Universal studios and a few other treats.

For months prior to the departure we plotted and planned our days, I had booked Business class seats not because we where been lush, but I was not sure how my body would react to a ten-hour flight and our last holiday, Almeria Spain, the flight was three and a half hours, I got very bad spasm's because of the seats, our seats where the first as you got on and because there was a bulk head in front of us, the table for drinks/food etc. came out of the arm rest which now meant the already small 17 inch seat was now reduced by 2 inches to 15 inches.

After 2 hours, I was in a lot of pain, I tried stand only to find the curvature of the plane prevented that, so I had to straggle Claire as she sat, it was all very awkward, yet quickly forgotten once we arrived at the hotel, it was a hotel we had used previously and was pretty good for my disability but one day Claire was out sunning herself whilst I had returned to the room, I was feeling tired and decided to have a nap.

I lay on the bed but could not get comfortable, my own bed I can raise the back or the legs up and down as I can't really lay on my side and as I squirmed around trying to get a comfy position, I suddenly realised the double bed was not a double but 2 singles pushed together and they started to part, I knew there was no point trying to fight it, so as I slowly descended to the floor I managed to pull a couple of pillows with me, well there was no reason to be uncomfortable.

I struggled for about an hour trying to get back up but when a complete half of your body does not work, it's very difficult, it amazes me for example when I lift my stroke arm with my good arm, how much it weighs, eventually I heard the click of the door as Claire inserted the door card, she entered and went apeshit.

It isn't that she's mad at me, she gets upset because it highlights my condition and reminds us all how vulnerable I am, eventually I got back up onto my feet but the holiday was tainted and it left a bad taste in our mouths, the journey home was horrible and as we eventually got back to the airport carpark Claire headed off to the car, carrying all the bags whilst I slowly made my way up the middle of the road, as it was the flattest path for me, I heard the car start the lights turned on and before I knew it they were heading straight at me, at speed, eventually they moved to the side and the car pulled up alongside me, the window dropped down and a tired frustrated wife just screamed at me "What the hell are you doing in the middle of the road, for god's sake just get in the car".

The journey home was very quiet.

So back to my original point how was I going to react to a 10-hour flight.

It didn't start well and we hadn't even got on the plane, we arrived at Dublin airport and approached the desk.

"Passport and boarding cards please", the lady asked.

"I have passports but the website wouldn't let me down load to boarding cards" "No problem" she replied "Can I have your US Esta's?" I looked at her with a blank face "We need the Esta visa's before we can proceed", she said.

   I didn't have them, I looked across to see that look of disapproval from Claire, "I'm sorry" the lady continued "we cannot let you on the flight without your US Esta paperwork"

She then pointed over to some computer terminals and told us to fill in the required data and print the Esta's off.

We went over to the computers, both of us were grumpy, I had filled in some details after booking the flight at home but thought we would fill in the entry cards as we had last time we went state side, only problem was that was over ten years ago and technology had moved on.

It didn't help that the Aer Lingus computer was an early 18th century model and kept freezing and after spending 20 minutes imputing all Claire's details the dam thing froze and we lost all the data.

At this point I just said "Right, let's just forget this stupid idea of thinking that we could go on holiday without a problem, let's just go home".

I caught the look in Claire's eye, it was very close to agreeing with me but she said "Right, one more try and if it doesn't work, we go home"

Eventually it worked, after about an hour and a half we had the correct paper work and we got our boarding cards.

Whilst all this was going on I kept checking to see where my wheel chair was. The guy kept saying "I'll give you a call as soon as it arrives"

Instead of been able to have booked in and then relax in the Business class lounge, we found ourselves running late, so no time to wait for the wheelchair, Claire grabbed all the bags and we headed off to the departure gate, we got through security and eventually got to US Immigration, by this time we were both sweaty and disheveled and I was also in quite a bit of pain.

There were three Air Lingus Stewardess's in front of us, they could see we were somewhat distressed as departure time got closer and closer, and I feared we would miss our flight, one of the girls enquired if all was well, I told her how the wheelchair had not turned up and to be honest the day up until then had been fairly shite, "What flight are you on" she asked, we told her and she smiled "That's our flight, so don't worry it won't be leaving without us", they moved us in with themselves then one by one they disappeared through immigration, our turn arrived, passports were checked and before we knew it we were through and heading onto the plane, I had travelled many times to America but as I entered the air craft I was always shown to the right and down to Economy class, this was my first time at been directed to the left, and we walked into the business class section, what a difference the three center seats replaced by what I can only describe as a two person cockpit giving me more space than I ever have had on an aircraft, it soon became apparent that 10 hrs. on this plane was going to be a doddle.

We sat down, smiling from ear to ear looking at each other and giggling like school children, all of a sudden we were brought back to adulthood as a soft and gentle voice said "Would sir and madam like a drink", we both looked up to see the lovely stewardess who had come to our aid earlier standing beside us, a silver tray on which stood two bubbling glasses of champagne, Claire let out a deep breath "Oh, yes please" as she took the glass of bubbly offered, we chinked our glasses together sat back in our comfortable soft seats and sipped our libation whilst the tension of the previous three hours slipped from our bodies with two or three deep sighs.

The next three weeks were and we both agreed, the best three weeks of our lives, it took a stroke before the two of us realised life was for living and not just for working, our parents and our parents, parents had struggled and worked to a manner that now meant we could enjoy our lives, don't get me wrong we were and Claire still is, a very hard worker but I was one of those people who when we had a big snow storm still made it 30 miles into work whilst others living 2 miles away didn't.

When I say the next three weeks were the best of my life, I think it mainly came down to the way the States consider access and facilities for people with disabilities in a way I had never seen before, when we went to universal parks there was a choice of wheelchair or mobility scooter, the rides had a simulated seating position outside the ride so you could check if it suited your disability before wasting time queuing, the ground under foot was as flat as it could be, we travelled on to Las Vegas and the MGM Grand every carpet joint was seamless, the shops were set out in such a way that I could stay on the mobility scooter and browse the products, all of a sudden I just felt completely normal again, my disability right deep into the back of my thoughts.

Vegas was just the craziest place I have ever seen; it really is 24 hrs. nonstop.

Ok you can blow a lot of money in a short time if your dumb enough to do it, but you can also make it work for you, an example, myself and Claire played together not as 2 individuals, we had 50 dollars and played craps for about three hours sometimes winning and sometimes loosing and eventually the 50 dollars was gone, but with that 50 dollars we had three hours of really good entertainment, had met and chatted with other folks at the table, had drank 10 bottles of Bud light (2.5 pints each) which were complimentary as long as you were playing, so to sum up 3 hours entertainment, 80 dollars' worth of beer, good company, all for 50 Bucks'

One night we were playing craps, which is not the easiest game to play, it took a good few hours of study on you tube to figure it out, but anyway this night I said to Claire that I was getting a bit hungry, she agreed and off we went picking out one of the lovely restaurants in the hotel and it was only as we sat down we realised it was not 8.00pm in the evening but nearly 1.30am in the morning, that is how timeless Vegas is.

There is a darker seedier side to the strip, we headed out one evening to go down to the Bellagio Hotel as they have a fantastic water and light display and as I was walking down the strip I noticed some girls in what I thought were revealing super hero costumes like wonder woman and super girl, it was only as we got right up to them that I realised it was body paint and apart from a very small pair of bikini bottoms they were in the nip, now to be fair, they just stood there and guys had their photos taken with them, they did not try to accost you as you passed by but all the same it was a strange occurrence for a fella from the West of Ireland, ex-service men from America's armed forces were pitched along the strip with hats or boxes left in front for change, again they did not bother you but it was sad to see.

I'm not saying the Vegas strip is the safest place in the world but the cops and the judicial service come down very very hard on anyone who threatens the reputation of the strip, some rate it safety wise as good as Disney.

We then took a road trip in a Dodge Charger, probably not the same standard as the 1960's but it's still considered a muscle car, we headed to Hoover Dam, an incredible piece of engineering and then carried on to our main destination The Grand Canyon, Oh boy…. What an incredible bit of natural sculpture, it totally blew me away, far exceeding anything I could have dreamt off.

You can see it on TV or in magazines but nothing and I mean nothing can prepare you for the magnificence of this natural phenomenon and if any of you guys plan to go, one tip I give is to enter the park as early as you can, as the early sun causes colors and shadows that only nature can produce, then as you get towards mid-day the colors seem to change before your very eyes, it is mind boggling.

I suppose writing this book has made me look back on my life and whilst doing this I realized I had lived through one of the biggest changes in the history of mankind due to Silicon Valley, as a youth if I needed some information on a particular item, I got on a bus, travelled into Birmingham city center, walked for twenty minutes in order to reach the library then once in the library find the area of my subject maybe in the small card filing cabinets or by micro fiche, locate the book then read it until I reached the information I needed, or maybe I was in town dropping off a roll of film from my recent holiday, the holiday I found by reading through loads of holiday brochures and 3 hours in Thomas Cook booking it, eventually I reach the chemist drop off the roll of film, then return 3 days later to pick up my photos…. Maybe it was Christmas time and I had a voucher for HMV music, I go in, I find the Bruce Springsteen double album, the one I've been waiting 2 months to buy, it is absolutely incredible, it has a, wait for it, a whopping 23 tracks on it, they place it into a plastic bag and I head home on the bus reading the sleeve notes over and over again, I reach home and want to be able to listen to my album on the move, I have to record it in real time on to a cassette tape, now I can listen to it in the car or with my Walkman I can listen to it anywhere.

The Walkman or as it was originally named 'The Sound About' was released in July 1979, measured 4" X 5" and an inch thick, weighing just under 1lb and originally cost $128 which would be over $400 today.

In the Eighties, I paid £60.00, 3 weeks' wages for an LCD watch, not like the earlier digital watches where you had to push a button on the side to see the display, my one had a permanent display with two buttons on the side, one was for a back light for night use, the other one, the first push gave me a read out in seconds, the second push gave me the date.

I was at a Birmingham city game, they were playing Leeds united, I had my new watch on it was the same day that I had bought it.

As we queued to get into the ground it became obvious we would not be in for kick off, so we left and went to the turnstiles for the away fans, it was much quieter and soon we were in, but, surrounded by Leeds fans, myself and my friends were at an age where we didn't carry scarfs, so the idea was to watch the game then at half time try and get across to the Birmingham fans and our friends.

In all there was four of us and one lad Dave H had a reputation of been the Rodney of the group, the Birmingham players ran out onto the pitch to a raucous cheer from the home fans whilst again we just kept quiet.

2 minutes into the game, Kenny Burns, the Birmingham city striker scores a scorcher of a goal, nobody in the away end utters a word…… wait for it…. Apart from Dave H who screams his head off whilst jumping up and down, we grabbed him trying to subdue his celebrations, looking around I could see hundreds of eyes looking at us, and a snorting sound not dissimilar to that made by a pissed off Bull, within seconds they were down on us, boots from the right, boots from the left as I rolled about in this valley of death, one of my pals got hold of me and was dragging me to safety and it was then I saw it, well actually I didn't see it, and that was the problem, my watch, my 60 pound LCD digital watch was no longer on my wrist, I

shook the grip from my friend and dived headlong into the Leeds fans, I was on my hands and knees desperately searching for my precious piece of technical brilliance, then like the way you spot a shooting star from the corner of your eye as it crosses the night sky, I saw a glint, I turned to look and there it was, my watch, on the ground no more than four feet from me, I scrambled, completely oblivious to the number of kicks I received, I had tunnel vision and my watch was my only interest.

At last it was in my hand, I started laughing out loud delighted in my success, only to feel a tightness around my collar as two police officers hauled me back up to my feet, gave me a couple of slaps around the head, each one getting harder and harder as my laughing continued, frog marched me to a gate, opened it and threw me into the bosom of the Birmingham supporters.

My friends spread the tale around my local pub, how the crazy Jon McGinley dived into a bunch of Leeds fans and laughed at them as they set about me, I delighted in my new-found fame and never told them about my watch.

Now in my house I have the Amazon Alexa, a device that respond to my voice, I can ask it the time and it will tell me, anytime, anywhere in the world, it will tell me jokes, play games with me, what am I trying to say?....... Anybody from my era, we are the last of the predigital age, my Walkman could take a C120 tape, approx. 36 songs, a camera that could take 36 photos….. Now it seems endless, technology of the future is going to be interesting, I hope I'm around to see it

So, that's about it, life number 2 is going to continue I hope for many more years, it took a stroke before I realised life is short, so please don't let it run away on you, grab it, enjoy it and make as many memories as you can, thank you for reading my book, I hope you enjoyed it, is there time for another one??? We'll see.

A final thank you to Claire Mullins from Tuam, who corrected some of my atrocious spelling and tutored me in the spelling of Beans, been, being and beanz.

I bring you right up to date, today is the 10th March, 14.45pm I am about to hit the button that sends my near two year project to the publisher's never to be altered again, I am going to have a little rest, then pop to the offy (off license) get a couple of beers from Joe, a takeaway from the Emperors Palace, Tuam, feet up in front of the TV with my wife and watch the Ireland Vs Wales rugby match.

Gratefully yours

Jon McGinley

Aged 56 $_{3/4}$

Printed in Great Britain
by Amazon